William Gilpin

An essay on prints

William Gilpin

An essay on prints

ISBN/EAN: 9783742867193

Manufactured in Europe, USA, Canada, Australia, Japa

Cover: Foto ©Thomas Meinert / pixelio.de

Manufactured and distributed by brebook publishing software
(www.brebook.com)

William Gilpin

An essay on prints

AN

ESSAY

ON

PRINTS.

By WILLIAM GILPIN, M. A.
VICAR OF BOLDRE, NEAR LYMINGTON.

THIRD EDITION.

LONDON:
PRINTED BY G. SCOTT,
FOR R. BLAMIRE, STRAND; SOLD BY B. LAW, AVE-
MARY-LANE; AND R. FAULDER, NEW BOND STREET.
MDCCLXXXI.

TO THE HONOURABLE

HORACE WALPOLE,

IN DEFERENCE TO HIS TASTE

IN THE POLITE ARTS,

AND THE

VALUABLE RESEARCHES HE HAS MADE

TO IMPROVE THEM,

THE FOLLOWING WORK

IS INSCRIBED BY

HIS MOST OBEDIENT

AND VERY

HUMBLE SERVANT,

WILLIAM GILPIN.

PREFACE

TO THE

THIRD EDITION.

THE chief intention of the Author in the following work, was to put the elegant amusement of collecting prints, upon a more rational footing ; and to give the unexperienced collector a few principles to assist him.

With this view he thought it necessary to apply the principles of painting to prints : and as his observations, in this part of his work, are not always new, he hath at least made them concise.

His

His account of artists might easily have been inlarged, by having recourse to books: particularly, he could have availed himself much of the ingenious researches of Mr. WALPOLE : *but he did not chuse to swell his volume by what others had said so much better than he could do; but to rest merely on such observations as he had himself made.*

Of modern prints the author hath purposely said little; declining generally to give his opinion, especially if unfavourable, of living artists. But tho he thought himself not at liberty to find fault, he thought he might occasionally take an opportunity to commend. This however, he finds, has given offence. He can only say, that he meant not by praising one, to

imply

*imply inferiority in another; but, with-
out confidering the matter deeper, merely
illuftrated his fubjeEts with fuch prints, as
occurred to his memory.*

*After the firft edition of this work, the
author had an opportunity of feeing, in
the King's library, a very noble colleEtion
of* HOLLAR'S *works; and after the
fecond, another in the library of the
Duchefs Dowager of Portland. Upon
a review of thefe two vaft colleEtions of
the works of this very laborious artift,
the author thinks he might have faid
fomething more in his commendation. Befides the praife due to him for his fowls,
muffs, fhells, and butterflies, there is great
merit in many of his other works. The
gothic*

gothic ornaments of his cathedrals are often elegantly touched ; and sometimes even with freedom. The sword of ED-WARD VI. *the cup of* ANDREA MON-TEGNA, *and the vases from* HOLBEIN, are all beautiful. Many of his small views also are elegant, and pleasing. His distances are generally fine : in his foregrounds he is most deficient. Among these views is a beautiful one of London-Bridge, and the parts adjacent, taken somewhere near Somerset-House.—His loose etchings are far from wanting spirit. Two or three pieces of dead game, slightly touched, are very masterly: they are drawn with accuracy, and executed with freedom.—There is a beautiful piece of dead game too, among his high-finished prints :

prints: the group confifts of a hare hanging up, and a bafket of birds.—But
HOLLAR appears no where to more advantage, than in his imitations; particularly in his prints after Count GAUDE,
CALLOT, and BARLOW: he has admirably hit off the manner of thefe mafters;
of CALLOT efpecially, whofe beggars
have all the fpirit of the originals, in a
reduced fize.

At the fame time, we muft add, that
his works abound with many bad prints,
probably the firft efforts of his genius.
His fhipping, his large views, his fables,
his Ephefian matron, and many others are
very bad: his Virgil and Juvenal are
below criticifm.

The

The author only wishes to add, that when he speaks positively *in any part of the following work, he means not to speak* arbitrarily : *but only to avoid the tedious repetition of qualifying phrases.*

N. B. When the figures, on the *right hand* are spoken of, those are meant, which are opposite to the spectator's right hand ; and so of the left.

Explanation of Terms.

Composition : in its *large* sense, means a picture in general : in its *limited* one, the art of grouping figures, and combining the parts of a picture. In this latter sense, it is synonymous with *Disposition.*

Design : in its *strict* sense, applied chiefly to *drawing :* in its *more enlarged* one, defined page 3 : in its *most enlarged* one, sometimes taken for a picture in general.

A whole : The idea of *one* object, which a picture should give in its comprehensive view.

Expression :

Expreſſion : its *ſtriƈt* meaning defined page 24: but it often means the force by which objeƈts of *any* kind are reprefented.

Effeƈt : arifes chiefly from the management of light; but the word is fometimes applied to the general view of a piƈture.

Spirit : in its *ſtriƈt* fenfe, defined p. 34; but it is fometimes taken in a more *enlarged* one, and means the *general* effeƈt of a mafterly performance.

Manner : fynonymous with *Execution.*

Piƈturefque: a term expreſſive of that peculiar kind of beauty, which is agreeable in a piƈture.

Piƈturefque

Picturesque grace: an agreeable form given, in a picture, to a clownish figure.

Repose, or *Quietness* : applied to a picture when the *whole* is harmonious; when nothing glares either in the light, shade, or colouring.

To *keep down, take down,* or *bring down :* signify throwing a degree of shade upon a glaring light.

A middle tint : a medium between a strong light, and strong shade: the phrase in this work, is rarely expressive of colour.

Catching lights : strong lights, which strike upon some particular parts of an object, the rest of which is in shadow.

Studies :

Studies : the sketched ideas of a painter, not compleated.

Freedom : the result of quick execution.

Extremities : hands and feet.

Air : expresses chiefly the graceful action of the head ; but often means a graceful attitude.

Contrast : the opposition of one part to another.

THE

THE
CONTENTS.

CHAPTER I.

*The principles of Painting confidered, fo
far as they relate to prints.*

Painting, or picture, is diftinguifhed from a print only by
the colouring, and the man-
ner of execution. In other refpects, the
foundation of beauty is the fame in
both; and we confider a print, as we
do a picture, in a double light, with
regard to the *whole,* and with regard to

its

its *parts*. It may have an agreeable effeɛt as a *whole*, and yet be very culpable in its *parts*. It may be likewife the
reverfe. A man may make a good appearance upon the *whole*; tho his *limbs*,
examined feparately, may be wanting
in exaɛt proportion. His *limbs* on the
other hand, may be exaɛtly formed, and
yet his perfon, upon the *whole*, may be
difgufting.

To make a print agreeable as a *whole*,
a juft obfervance of thofe rules is neceffary, which relate to *defign, difpofition,
keeping*, and the *diftribution of light:* to
make it agreeable in its *parts*—of thofe
which relate to *drawing, expreffion, grace,*
and *perfpeɛtive*.

We confider the *whole* before its
parts, as it naturally precedes in practice. The painter firft forms his general
ideas;

ideas; and difpofes them, yet crude, in fuch a manner, as to receive the moft beautiful form, and the moft beautiful effect of light. His laft work is to fi- nifh the feveral parts: as the ftatuary fhapes his block, before he attempts to give delicacy to the limbs.

By *defign*, (a term which painters fometimes ufe in a more limited fenfe) we mean the general conduct of the piece, as a reprefentation of fuch a par- ticular ftory. It anfwers, in an hiftori- cal relation of a fact, to a judicious choice of circumftances; and includes a *proper time, proper characters,* the *moft affecting manner of introducing thofe cha- racters,* and *proper appendages.*

With regard to a *proper time,* the painter is affifted by good old dramatic rules; which inform him, that *one* point

of

of time only fhould be taken—the moft affecting in the action; and that no other part of the ftory fhould interfere with it. Thus *in the death of* ANANIAS, if the inftant of his falling down be chofen, no anachronifm fhould be introduced; every part of the piece fhould correfpond; each character fhould be under the ftrongeft impreffion of aftonifhment, and horror : thofe paffions being yet unallayed by any cooler paffions fucceeding.

With regard to *characters,* the painter muft fuit them to his piece, by attending to hiftorical truth, if his fubject be hiftory; or to heathen mythology, if it be fabulous.

He muft alfo *introduce them properly.* They fhould be ordered in fo advantageous a manner, that the principal figures,

figures, thofe which are moft concerned
in the action, fhould catch the eye *firft*,
and engage it *moft*. This is very effential in a well-told ftory. In the firft
place, they fhould be the leaft embarraf-
fed of the group. This alone gives
them diftinction. But they may be farther diftinguifhed, fometimes by a *broad
light*; fometimes by a *ftrong fhadow*, in
the midft of a light; fometimes by a
remarkable *action*, or *expreffion*; and
fometimes by a combination of two or
three of thefe modes of diftinction.

The laft thing included in *defign* is
the ufe of *proper appendages*. By *appendages* are meant animals, landfkip, buildings, and in general, what-ever is introduced into the piece by way of ornament. Every thing of this kind fhould
correfpond with the fubject, and rank

in

in a proper fubordination to it. BAS-
SAN would fometimes paint a fcripture-
ftory; and his method was, to croud
his fore-ground with cattle: while
you feek for his principal figures,
and at length with difficulty find them
in fome remote corner of his picture.
We often fee a landfkip well adorned with a ftory in miniature. The
landfkip here is principal; but at the
fame time, the figures, which tell the
ftory, tho fubordinate to the landfkip, are the *principal figures*. BAS-
SAN's practice was different. In his pictures neither the *landfkip*, nor the *ftory*
is principal; but his cattle. To introduce a ftory is abfurd.

When all thefe rules are obferved,
when a proper point of time is chofen;
when characters correfponding with the
subject

fubject are introduced, and thefe ordered fo judicioufly as to point out the ftory in the ftrongeft manner; and laftly,
when all the appendages, and under-
parts of the piece are fuitable, and fub-
fervient to the fubject ; then the ftory is
well told, and of courfe the *defign* is
perfect.

The fecond thing to be confidered
with regard to a *whole*, is *difpofition*. By
this word is meant the art of grouping
the figures, and of combining the feveral parts of a picture. *Defign* confiders
how each part, *feparately taken*, concurs,
in producing a *whole*;— a *whole*, arifing
from the *unity of the fubject*, not the *effect of the object*. For the figures in a
piece may be fo ordered, as to tell the
ftory in an affecting manner, which is

B 4

as

as far as *defign* goes; and yet may want that agreeable *combination*, which is neceffary to pleafe the eye. To produce fuch a combination is the bufinefs of *difpofition*. In the cartoon of St. PAUL *preaching at Athens*, the *defign* is perfect; and the characters in particular, are fo ordered, as to tell the ftory in a very affecting manner: yet the feveral parts of the picture are far from being agreeably combined. If RUBENS had had the *difpofition* of the materials of this picture, its effect as a *whole* had been very different.

Having thus diftinguifhed between *defign* and *difpofition*, I fhall explain the latter a little farther.

It is an obvious principle, that one object at a time is enough to engage either the fenfes, or the intellect. Hence the

ne neceffity of *unity*, or a *whole*, in painting. The eye, upon a complex view,
muft be able to comprehend the picture
as *one object*, or it cannot be fatisfied.
It may be pleafed indeed by feeding on
the parts feparately: but a picture,
which can pleafe no otherwife, is as
poor a production as a machine; whofe
fprings and wheels are finifhed with
nicety, but are unable to act in concert,
and effect the intended movement.

. Now *difpofition*, or the art of grouping and combining the figures, and feveral parts of a picture, contributes
greatly to make the picture appear as
one object. When the parts are fcattered, they have no dependance on
each other; they are ftill only parts:
but when, by an agreeable grouping,
they

they are maffed together, they become a *whole.*

In difpofing figures, great artifice is neceffary to make each group open it-felf in fuch a manner, as to fet off advantageoufly the feveral figures, of which it is compofed. The *action* at leaft of each figure fhould appear.

No group can be agreeable without *contraft.* By *contraft* is meant the oppofition of one part to another. A famenefs in attitude, action, or expreffion, among figures in the fame group, will always difguft the eye. In the cartoon of St. PAUL *preaching at Athens,* the contraft among the figures is incomparably fine; and the want of it, *in the death of* ANANIAS, makes the group of the apoftles a difagreeable one.

Nor

Nor indeed is *contraſt* required only
among the *figures* of the *ſame* group,
but alſo among the *groups themſelves*,
and among *all the parts*, of which the
piece is compoſed. In the *beautiful gate
of the temple*, the figures of the principal
group are very well contraſted; but the
adjoining group is diſpoſed almoſt in
the ſame manner; which, together with
the formal pillars, introduce a diſagreeable regularity into the picture.

The judicious painter, however, whether he group, combine, or contraſt,
will always avoid the *appearance of artifice*. The ſeveral parts of his picture
will be ſo ſuited to each other, that his
art will ſeem the reſult of chance. In
the *ſacrifice at Lyſtra*, the head of the ox
is bowed down, with a deſign, no
doubt, to group the figures around it
more

more harmonioufly: but their action is fo well fuited to the pofture of the ox, and the whole managed with fo much judgment, that, altho the figures are difpofed with the utmoft art, they appear with all the eafe of nature. The remaining part of the group is an inftance of the reverfe; in which a number of heads appear manifeftly ftuck in to fill up vacuities.

But farther, as a *whole,* or *unity,* is an effential of beauty, *that difpofition* is certainly the moft perfect, which admits but of *one* group. All fubjects, howeever, will not allow this *clofe* obfervance of unity. When this is the cafe, the feveral groups muft again be combined; chiefly by a proper diftribution of light, fo as to conftitute a *whole.*

But

But as the *whole* will foon be loft, if the conftituent *parts* become *numerous,* it follows, that *many* groups muft not be admitted. Judicious painters have thought *three* the utmoft number, that can be allowed. Some fubjects indeed, as battles and triumphs, neceffarily require a great number of figures, and of courfe various combinations of groups. In the management of *fuch* fubjects, the greateft art is neceffary to preferve a *whole.* Confufion in the figures muft be expreffed without confufion in the picture. A writer fhould treat his fubject *clearly,* tho he write upon *obfcurity.*

With regard to *difpofition,* I fhall only add, that the *fhape* or *form* of the group fhould alfo be confidered. The *triangular* form MICHAEL ANGELO thought the moft beautiful. And in-
indeed

deed there is a lightneſs in it, which no other form can receive. The group of the apoſtles, in the cartoon of *giving the keys,* and the ſame group, in the *death of* ANANIAS, are both exceedingly heavy; and this heavineſs ariſes from nothing more than from the form of a parallelogram, within the lines of which theſe groups are contained. The triangular form too is capable of the moſt variety: for the verticle angle of a group ſo diſpoſed may either be acute, or obtuſe, in any degree. Or a *ſegment* only of a triangle may be taken, which ſtill encreaſes the variety. But it muſt be obſerved, that to make a triangular form beautiful, a perpendicular from the apex ſhould fall upon the baſe. The cartoons afford few inſtances of beauty in the *forms* of *groups.* In the

works

works of SALVATOR ROSA we frequently find them.

The painter, when he hath chofen his
fubject, fhould always fketch out fome
beautiful form of grouping, which may
beft fuit it; within which bounds he
fhould, as nearly as may be, without
affectation, confine his figures. What I
mean, is, that the *form* of the group
fhould never be left at random.

A third thing to be confidered in a
picture, with regard to a *whole*, is *keeping*. This word implies the different
degrees of ftrength and faintnefs, which
objects receive from nearnefs and diftance. A nice obfervance of the gra-
dual fading of light and fhade contributes greatly towards the production of
a *whole*. Without it, the diftant parts,
instead

inftead of being connected with the objects at hand, appear like foreign objects, wildly introduced, and without
meaning. Diminifhed in *fize* only, they
put you in mind of Lilliput and Brob-
dignag united in one fcene. *Keeping* is
generally found in great perfection in
DELLA BELLA's prints : and the want of
it, as confpicuoufly in TEMPESTA's.

Nearly allied to *keeping* is the doc-
trine of *harmony*, which equally contributes towards the production of a *whole*.
In *painting*, it has amazing force. A
judicious arrangement of according tints
will ftrike even the unpracticed eye.
The *effect* of every picture, in a great
meafure, depends on one principal and
mafter-tint ; which, like the key-tone in
mufic, prevails over the whole piece.
Sometimes

Sometimes the purple tint is chofen: fometimes the mellow, brown one; and in fome fubjects the greenifh hue is moft proper. Of this ruling tint, whatever it is, every object in the picture fhould in a degree participate. This theory is founded on principles of truth; and produces a fine effect from the *harmony,* in which it unites every object. Harmony is oppofed to gaudy colouring, and glare. Yet the fkilful painter fears not, when his fubject allows it, to employ the greateft variety of rich tints; and tho he may depreciate their value in fhadow, he will not fcruple in his lights, to give each its utmoft glow. His art lies deeper. He takes the glare from one vivid tint by introducing another; and from a nice affemblage of the brighteft colours, each of which a-

C   lone

lone would ftare, he creates an united glow in the higheft degree harmonious. He refolves even the moft difcordant tints into union, and makes them fub-fervient to his grand effect; as the able mufician will often dare to introduce notes foreign to his key; and even from apparent difcord derive exquifite har-mony. But thefe great effects of har-mony are only to be produced by the magic of colours. The harmony of a print is a more fimple production : and yet unlefs a print be harmonized by the fame *tone of fhadow*, if I may fo exprefs myfelf, there will always appear a great deficiency in it. We often meet with hard touches in a print; which, ftand-ing alone, are unharmonious : but when every contiguous part is touched-up to that *tone*, the effect is harmony.—*Keep-*

ing

ing then proportions a proper degree ot ftrength to the near and diftant parts, in refpect to *each other*. *Harmony* goes a ftep farther, and keeps each part quiet, with refpect to itfelf, and the *whole*. I fhall only add, that in fketches, and rough etchings, no *harmony* is expected: it is enough, if *keeping* be obferved. *Harmony* is looked for only in finifhed compofitions. If you would fee the want of it in the ftrongeft light, exa-mine a worn-print, harfhly retouched by fome bungler.

The laft thing, which contributes to produce a *whole*, is a proper *diftribution of light*. This, in a print efpecially, is moft effential. Harmony in colouring may, in fome meafure, fupply its place in painting: but a print has no fucce-

C 2   daneum,

daneum. Were the *defign, difpofition,* and *keeping* ever fo perfect, beautiful, and juft; without this effential, inftead of a whole, we fhould have only a piece of patch-work. Nay, fuch is the power of *light,* that by an artificial management of it we may even harmonize a bad difpofition.

The general rule which regards the diftribution of *light,* is, that it fhould be fpread in *large maffes.* This gives the idea of a *whole.* Every grand object catches the light only upon one large furface. Where the light is in fpots, we have the idea of feveral objects; or at leaft of an incoherent one, if the object be fingle; which the eye furveys with difficulty. It is thus in painting. When we fee, upon a *comprehenfive* view, *large maffes* of light and

fhade,

shade, we have, of course, the idea of a *whole*—of *unity* in that picture. But where the light is scattered, we have the idea of several objects, or at least of one broken and confused. TITIAN's known illustration of this point by a bunch of grapes is beautiful, and explanatory. When the light falls upon the *whole bunch* together (one side being illumined, and the other dark) we have the representation of those large masses, which constitute a *whole*. But when the grapes are stripped from the bunch, and scattered upon a table (the light shining upon each separately) a *whole* is no longer preserved.

Having thus considered those essentials of a print, which produce a *whole*, it remains to consider those, which relate

late

late to the *parts—drawing, expreſſion,
grace,* and *perſpective.* With regard to
theſe, let it be firſt obſerved, that in order, they are inferior to the other. The
production of a *whole* is the great effect,
that ſhould be aimed at in a picture.
A picture without a *whole* is properly
only a ſtudy: and thoſe things, which
produce a *whole,* are of courſe the *principal* foundation of beauty. So thought
the great maſter of compoſition. With
him no man was intitled to the name of
artiſt, who could not produce a *whole.*
However exquiſitely he might finiſh, he
would ſtill be defective. *Infelix operis
ſummâ, quia ponere totum neſciet.*

By *drawing* we mean the exactneſs of
the out-line. Without a competent
knowledge of this there can be no juſt
repre-

reprefentation of nature. Every thing
will be diftorted and offenfive to the
eye. *Bad* drawing therefore is that difgufting object which no eye can bear.

Drawing, however, may be very tolerable, though it fall fhort, in a *certain
degree*, of abfolute perfection. The defect will only be obferved by the moft
critical, and anatomical eye: and we
may venture to fay, that drawing is
ranked too high, when the *niceties* of it
are confidered in preference to thofe effentials, which conftitute a *whole*.

Expreffion is the life and foul of painting. It implies a juft reprefentation of
paffion, and of *character*: of *paffion*, by
exhibiting every emotion of the mind,
as outwardly difcovered by any peculi-
arity of gefture ; or the extention, and

con-

contraction of the features: of *character*, by representing the different manners of men, as arising from their particular tempers, or professions. The cartoons are full of examples of the first kind of *expression*; and with regard to the second, commonly called *manners-painting*, it would be invidious not to mention our countryman HOGARTH ; whose works contain a variety of characters, *represented* with more force, than most men can *conceive.*

Grace consists in such a disposition of the parts of a figure, as forms it into an agreeable attitude. It depends on *contrast* and *ease*. *Contrast*, when applied to a single figure, means the same, as when applied to a group; the opposition of one part to another. It may be
considered

confidered with reference to the *body*, the *limbs*, and the *head*; the graceful attitude arifing fometimes from a contraft in one, fometimes in another, and fometimes in all. With reference to the *body*, contraft confifts in giving it an eafy turn, oppofing concave parts to convex. Of this, St. PAUL in *the facrifice at Lyftra* is an inftance.—With reference to the *limbs*, it confifts in the oppofition between extenfion and contraction. MICHAEL ANGELO's illuftration by a triangle, or pyramid, may here likewife again be introduced; this form giving grace and beauty to a *fingle figure*, as well as to a *group*. Only here a greater liberty may be allowed. In *grouping*, the triangle fhould, I think, always reft upon its bafe; but in a fingle figure, it may be inverted, and ftand upon its apex.

Thus

Thus if the lower parts of the figure be extended, the upper parts fhould be contracted; but the fame beautiful form is given by extending the arms, and drawing the feet to a point.—Laftly, contraft often arifes from the air of the head; which is given by a turn of the neck from the line of the body. The cartoons abound with examples of this fpecies of *grace*. It is very remarkable in the figure of St. John healing the cripple: and the fame cartoon affords eight or nine more inftances. I fay the lefs on this fubject, as it hath been fo well explained by the ingenious author of the *Analyfis of Beauty*.

Thus *contraft* is the foundation of *grace*; but it muft ever be remembred, that *contraft* fhould be accompanied with
eafe.

eafe. The body fhould be *turned*, not *twifted*; every *conftrained* pofture avoided; and every motion fuch, as nature, which loves eafe, would dictate.

What hath been faid on this head relates equally to *all* figures; thofe drawn from *low*, as well as thofe from *high* life. And here we may diftinguifh between *picturefque* grace, and that grace which arifes from *dignity of character.* Of the *former* kind, which is the kind here treated of, *all* figures fhould partake: you find it in BERGHEM's clowns, and in CALLOT's beggars: but it belongs to *expreffion* to mark thofe characteriftics, which diftinguifh the *latter*.

I fhall only obferve farther, that when the piece confifts of many figures, the contraft of *each fingle* figure fhould be fubordinate to the contraft of the *whole*.

It

It will be improper therefore, in many cafes, to practife the rules, which have been juft laid down. They ought, however, to be a general direction to the painter; and at leaft to be obferved in the *principal* figures.—If a *fingle* figure be introduced, as in portrait, the pyramidal form cannot well be difpenfed with : the *figure* partakes then of the nature of a *group*.

Perfpective is that proportion, with regard to *fize*, which near and diftant objects, with their parts, bear to each other. It is an attendant on *keeping*: one gives the out-line; and the other fills it up. Without a competent knowledge of *perfpective* very abfurd things would be introduced : and yet to make a vain fhew of it, is pedantic.——Under

der this head may be reduced *fore-fhort-ning*. Unlefs this be done with the ut-moft art, it were better omitted : it will otherwife occafion great aukwardnefs. RUBENS is famous for *fore-fhortning*; but the effect is chiefly feen in his *paintings*; feldom in his *prints*.

To this fummary of the rules, which relate to the *whole* of a picture, and to its *parts*, I fhall juft add a few obferva-tions upon *execution*; which relates e-qually to both.

By *execution* is meant that manner of working, by which each artift produces his effect. Artifts may differ in their *execution* or *manner*, and yet all excel. CALLOT, for inftance, ufes a ftrong, firm ftroke; SALVATOR, a flight, and loofe
one;

one; while REMBRANDT executes in a manner different from them both, by fcratches feemingly at random.

Every artift is in fome degree a *mannerift* : that is, he executes in a *manner* peculiar to himfelf. But the word *mannerift* has generally a clofer fenfe. Nature fhould be the ftandard of imitation: and every object fhould be executed, as nearly as poffible, in *her manner*. Thus SALVATOR's figures, DU JARDIN's animals, and WATERLO's landfkips, are all ftrongly impreffed with the character of nature. Other mafters again, deviating from this ftandard, inftead of nature, have recourfe only to their own ideas. They have gotten a general idea of a man, a horfe, or a tree; and to thefe ideas they apply upon all occafions. Inftead therefore of reprefenting

fenting that endlefs variety, which nature exhibits on every fubjeƈt, a famenefs runs through all their performances. Every figure, and every tree bears
the fame ftamp. Such artifts are *properly* called *mannerifts*. TEMPEST, CALLOT,
and TESTA are all *mannerifts* of this
kind. Their ideas are plainly no copies
from nature. PERELLE's landfkips too
are mere tranfcripts of imagination.—
The artift, however, who copies nature,
if he make a bad choice (as REMBRANDT
often did) is lefs agreeable than the *mannerift*; who gives us his own elevated
ideas, touched with fpirit and character, tho not with exaƈt truth. He is
the true artift, who copies nature; but,
where he finds her mean, elevates her
from his own ideas of beauty, which
have

have been treasured up from the same great original. Such was SALVATOR.

By the *spirit* and *freedom* of *execution*, we mean something, which it is difficult to explain. A certain heaviness always follows, when the artist is not sure of his stroke, and cannot execute his idea with precision. The reverse is the case, when he is certain of it, and gives it boldly. I know not how to explain better what is meant by *spirit*. Mere *freedom* a quick execution will give ; but unless that *freedom* be attended with precision, the stroke, however free, will be so unmeaning as to lose its effect.

To these observations, it may not be improper to add a short comparative view of the *peculiar* excellencies of
pictures

pictures, and prints; which will shew us, in what points the picture has the advantage.

In *design* and *composition* the effects of both are equal. The print exhibits them with as much force and meaning, as the picture.

In *keeping* the picture has the advantage. The *haziness* of distance cannot well be expressed by any thing but the *hue of nature*, which the pencil is very able to give. The print *endeavours* to preserve this haziness; and to give the idea: but does it imperfectly. It does little more than aid the memory. We know the appearance exists in nature : and the print furnishes an hint to recollect it.

D   In

In the *diſtribution of light* the com-
pariſon runs very wide. Here the painter avails himſelf of a thouſand varied
tints, which aſſiſt him in this buſineſs ;
and by which he can harmonize his
gradations from light to ſhade with an
almoſt infinite variéty. Harmonious colouring has in itſelf the effect of a proper diſtribution of light. The engraver, in the mean time, is left to work
out his effect with two materials only,
plain white and black.—In the print,
however, you can more eaſily trace
the *principles* of light and ſhade. The
pencil is the implement of deception;
and it requires the eye of a maſter
to diſtinguiſh between the effect of light,
and the effect of colour: but in the
print, even the unpractiſed eye can
readily catch the maſs; and follow the
diſtribution

diftribution of it through all its variety of middle tints.—One thing more may be added : If the picture has no harmony in its colouring, the tints being all at difcord among themfelves, which is often the cafe in the works even of reputable painters, a good print, from fuch a picture, is more beautiful than the picture itfelf. It preferves what is valuable, (upon a fuppofition there is any thing valuable in it) and removes what is offenfive.

Thus the comparifon runs with regard to thofe effentials, which relate to a *whole*: with regard to *drawing, expreffion, grace,* and *perfpective,* we can purfue it only in the two former: in the two latter, the picture and the print feem to have equal advantages.—With

regard

regard to *perfpective* indeed, the lines of the print verging all to one point, mark the *principles* of it more ftrongly.

Drawing, in a *picture*, is effected by the contiguity of two different colours : in a *print* by a pofitive line. In the *picture*, therefore, *drawing* has more of nature in it, and more of effect : but the ftudent in anatomy finds more precifion in the print; and can more eafily trace the line, and follow it in all its windings through light and fhade.— In mezzotinto the comparifon fails; in which, drawing is effected nearly as it is in painting.

With regard to *expreffion*, the painter glories in his many advantages. The paffions receive their force almoft as

much

much from *colour*, as from the emotion
of feature. Nay lines, without colour,
have frequently an effect very oppofite
to what is intended. Violent expreffions,
when lineal only, are often grotefque.
The complexion fhould fupport the dif-
tortion. The bloated eyes of immode-
rate grief degenerate into courfe features, unlefs the pencil add thofe high-
blown touches, which mark the paffion.
Afk the engraver, why he could not
give the dying faint of DOMINICHINO
his true expreffion?* Why he gave him
that ghaftly horrour, inftead of the fe-
rene langour of the original? The engraver may with juftice fay, he went as
far as lines could go; but he wanted
DOMINICHINO's pencil to give thofe pal-

* JAC FREII's copy of DOMINICHINO's St. *Jerome.*

lid

lid touches, which alone could make his lines expressive.—Age also, and sex, the bloom of youth, and the wan cheek of sickness, are equally indebted for their most characteristic marks, to the pencil.—In *portrait*, the different hues of hair, and complexion;—in *animal-life* the various dies of furs, and plumage;—in *landskip*, the peculiar tints of seasons; of morning, and evening; the light azure of a summer-sky; the sultry glow of noon; the bluish, or purple tinge, which the mountain assumes, as it recedes, or approaches; the grey moss upon the ruin; the variegated greens, and mellow browns of foliage, and broken ground: in short, the colours of every part of nature, have all amazing force in strengthening the expression of objects.—In the room

of

of all this, the deficient print has only
to offer mere form, and the gradations of fimple light. Hence the fweet
touches of the pencil of CLAUDE,
mark his pictures with the ftrongeft
expreffions of nature, and render them
invaluable; while his prints are generally the dirty fhapes of fomething,
which he could not exprefs.

The idea alfo of *diftant magnitude,*
the print gives very imperfectly. It
is expreffed chiefly by colour. Air,
which is naturally blue, is the medium through which we fee ; and every
object participates of this bluenefs.
When the diftance is fmall, the tinge
is imperceptible : as it increafes, the
tinge grows ftronger ; and when the
object is very remote, it intirely lofes

its

its natural colour, and becomes blue.
And indeed this is fo familiar a criterion of diftance, at leaft with thofe
who live in mountainous countries,
that if the object be vifible at all, after it has received the full *ether-tinge*,
if I may fo fpeak, the fight immediately judges it to be very large. The
eye ranging over the plains of Egypt,
and catching the blue point of a pyramid, from the colour concludes the
diftance; and is ftruck with the magnitude of an object, which, through fuch
a fpace, can exhibit form.—Here the
print fails : this criterion of diftant magnitude, it is unable to give.

I cannot forbear inferting here a fhort
criticifm on a paffage in VIRGIL. The
poet

poet defcribing a tower retiring from a veffel in full fail, fays,

Protinus aërias Phæacum abfcondimus arces.

Ruæus, and other commentators, explain *aërias* by *atlas*, or fome equivalent word; which is magnifying an idea which in nature fhould be diminifhed. The idea of magnitude is certainly not the ftriking idea that arifes from a retiring object: I fhould rather imagine that Virgil, who was of all poets perhaps the moft picturefque, meant to give us an idea of colour, rather than of fhape; and that the tower, from its diftance, had affumed the aerial tinge.

The print equally fails, when the medium itfelf receives a foreign tinge from a ftrength of colour behind it.

The

The idea of horrour, impreſſed by an expanſe of air glowing, in the night, with diſtant fire, cannot be raiſed by black and white. VANDERVELDE has contrived to give us a good idea of the dreadful glare of a fleet in flames: but it were ridiculous for an engraver to attempt ſuch a ſubject; becauſe he cannot expreſs that idea, which principally illuſtrates his ſtory.

Tranſparency is another thing, which the print is very unable to expreſs. It is the united tinge of two colours, one behind the other; each of which, in part, diſcovers itſelf ſingly. If you employ one colour only, you have the idea of opaqueneſs. A fine carnation is a white tranſparent ſkin, ſpread over a multitude of ſmall blood veſſels, which

bluſh

blufh through it. When the breath departs, thefe little fountains of life flow no longer; the bloom fades; and livid palenefs, the colour of death, fucceeds. —The happy pencil can mark both thefe effects. It can fpread the glow of health over the cheek of beauty; and it can with equal facility exprefs the cold, wan, tint of human clay. The print can exprefs neither; reprefenting, in the fame dry manner, the bright tranfparency of the one, and the inert opaquenefs of the other.

Laftly, the print fails in the expreffion of *polifhed bodies*; which are indebted for their chief luftre to *reflected colours.* The print indeed goes farther here, than in the cafe of tranfparency. In this it can do very little: in *polifhed bodies,*

bodies; it can at least give *reflected shapes.* It can shew the *forms* of hanging woods upon the edges of the lake; tho unable to give the kindred tinge. But in many cases the *polished* body receives the *tinge*, without the *shape*. Here the engraver is wholly deficient: he knows not how to stain the gleaming silver with the purple liquour it contains; nor is he able to give the hero's armour its highest polish from the tinge of the crimson vest, which covers it.

A single word upon the subject of *execution*, shall conclude these remarks. Here the advantage lies wholly on the side of painting. *That* manner which can best give the idea of the surface of an object, is the best; and the lines of the finest engraving are harsh in compa-
rison

rifon of the fmooth flow of the pencil. *Mezzotinto,* tho deficient in fome re-fpects, is certainly in others the happieft manner of execution; and the ancient *wooden print,* in which the middle tint is ufed; is undoubtedly, in point of exe-cution, beyond either etching or engrav-ing.

CHAP.

C H A P T E R II.

Obfervations on the different Kinds of Prints.

THERE are three kinds of prints, *engravings, etchings,* and *mezzotintos.* The characteriftic of the firft is *ftrength*; of the fecond, *freedom*; and of the third, *foftnefs.* All thefe, however, may in fome degree be found in each.

From the fhape of the engraver's tool, each ftroke is an angular incifion; which

which muft of courfe give the line ftrength, and firmnefs; if it be not very tender. From fuch a line alfo, as it is a deliberate one, correctnefs may be expected; but no great freedom: for it is a laboured line, ploughed through the metal, and muft neceffarily, in a degree, want eafe.

Unlimited *freedom*, on the other hand, is the characteriftic of *etching*. The needle, gliding along the furface of the copper, meets no refiftance; and eafily takes any turn the hand pleafes to give it. Etching indeed is mere drawing: and may be practifed with the fame facility.—But as *aqua-fortis* bites in an *equable* manner, it cannot give the lines that ftrength, which they receive from a pointed graver cutting into the copper.

per. Besides, it is difficult to prevent its biting the plate *all over* alike. The *distant parts* indeed may easily be covered with wax, and the *general* effect of, the *keeping* preserved; but to give each *smaller* part its proper relief, and to *harmonize* the *whole*, requires so many different degrees of strength, such easy transitions from one into another, that aqua-fortis alone is not equal to it. Here, therefore, engraving hath the advantage; which by a stroke, deep or tender, at the artist's pleasure, can vary strength and faintness in any degree.

As engraving, therefore, and etching have their respective advantages, and deficiencies, artists have endeavoured to unite their powers; and to correct the faults of each, by joining the *freedom* of

E   the

the one, with the *strength* of the other.
In moſt of our modern prints, the plate
is firſt etched, and afterwards ſtrength-
ened, and finiſhed by the graver. And
when this is *well* done, it has a happy
effect. The flatneſs, which is the con-
ſequence of an equable ſtrength of ſhade,
is taken off; and the print gains a new
effect, by the relief given to thoſe parts
which *hang* (in the painter's language)
upon the parts behind them.—But great
art is neceſſary in this buſineſs. We ſee
many a print, which wanted only a *few*
touches, when it appeared in its etched
proof, receive afterwards ſo *many*, as to
become laboured, heavy and diſguſt-
ing.

In *etching*, we have the greateſt variety
of excellent prints. The caſe is, it is

ſo

ſo much the ſame as *drawing*, that we
have the very works themſelves of the
moſt celebrated maſters: many of whom
have left behind them prints in this
way; which, however ſlight and incorrect, will always have ſomething *maſterly*, and of courſe *beautiful* in them.

In the muſcling of human figures,
of any conſiderable ſize, *engraving* hath
undoubtedly the advantage of *etching*.
The ſoft and delicate tranſitions, from
light to ſhade, which are there required, cannot be ſo well expreſſed by the
needle: and, in general, *large prints* require a ſtrength which *etching* cannot
give; and are therefore fit objects of *engraving*.

Etching, on the other hand, is more

E 2   par-

particularly adapted to fketches, and flight defigns: which, if executed by an engraver, would entirely lofe their freedom; and with it their beauty. Landfkip too, in general, is the object of *etching.* The foliage of trees, ruins, fky, and indeed every part of landfkip, requires the utmoft freedom. In finifh - ing an *etched* landfkip with the *tool,* (as it is called) too much care cannot be taken to prevent heavinefs. We re- marked before the nicety of touching upon an etched plate; but in landfkip the bufinefs is peculiarly delicate. The fore-grounds, and the boles of fuch trees as are placed upon them, may require a few ftrong touches; and here and there a few harmonizing ftrokes will add to the effect: but if the engraver

venture

venture much farther, he has good luck if he do no mifchief.

An *engraved* plate, unlefs it be cut very flightly, will caft off feven or eight hundred good impreffions: and yet this depends, in fome degree, upon the hardnefs of the copper. An *etched* plate will not give above two hundred; unlefs it be eaten very deep, and then it may perhaps give three hundred. After that, the plate muft be retouched, or the impreffions will be faint.

Befides the common method of engraving on *copper,* we have prints engraven on pewter, and on wood. The pewter plate gives a coarfenefs and dirtinefs to the print, which is often difagreeable. But engraving upon wood is

capable

capable of great beauty. Of this fpecies of engraving more fhall elfewhere
be faid.

Mezzotinto is very different from either *engraving* or *etching*. In thefe, you
make the *fhades*; in *mezzotinto*, the *lights*.
Since the time of its invention by
Prince RUPERT, as is commonly fuppofed, the art of fcraping *mezzotintos* is
greatly more improved than either of
its fifter-arts. Some of the earlieft *etchings* are perhaps the beft; and *engraving*, fince the times of GOLTZIUS and
MULLER, hath not perhaps made any
very great advances. But *mezzotinto,*
compared with its original ftate, is, at
this day, almoft a new art. If we exa-
mine fome of the modern pieces of
workmanfhip in this way; the *Jewifh*
Rabbi

Rabbi, the portrait of Mrs. Lascelles *with a child on her knee*, Mr. Garrick *between Tragedy and Comedy*; and feveral other prints equally good, by our beft mezzotinto-fcrapers; they as much exceed the works of White and Smith; as thofe mafters did Becket and Simons. It muft be owned, at the fame time, they have better originals to copy. Kneller's portraits are very paltry, compared with thofe of our modern artifts; and are fcarce fufceptible of any effects of light and fhade. As to Prince Rupert's works, I never faw any, which were *certainly* known to be his: but I make no doubt they were executed in the fame black, harfh, difagreeable manner, which appears fo ftrong in the mafters who fucceeded him. The invention however was noble; and the early

mafters

masters have the credit of it: but the truth is, the ingenious mechanic hath ᐧbeen called in to the painter's aid; and hath invented a manner of *laying ground*, wholly unknown to the earlier mas-ters: and they who are acquainted with *mezzotinto*, know the *ground* to be a very capital consideration.

The characteristic of *mezzotinto* is *soft-nefs*; which adapts it chiefly to portrait, or history, with a few figures, and thefe not too fmall. Nothing, except paint, can exprefs flefh more naturally, or the flowing of hair, or the folds of drapery, or the catching lights of armour. In engraving and etching we muft get over the prejudices of crofs lines, which exift on no natural bodies: but *mezzotinto* gives us the ftrongeft reprefentation of a *furface*. If, however, the figures are

too

too crowded, it wants ftrength to detach the feveral parts with a proper relief: and if they are very fmall, it wants
precifion, which can only be given by
an outline; or, as in painting, by a different tint. The unevennefs of the
ground will occafion bad drawing, and
aukwardnefs—in the extremities efpecially. Some inferior artifts have endeavoured to remedy this, by terminat-
ing their figures with an engraved, or
etched line: but they have tried the ex-
periment with bad fuccefs. The ftrength
of the line, and the foftnefs of the
ground, accord ill together. I fpeak
not here of that judicious mixture of
etching and *mezzotinto,* which was former-
ly ufed by WHITE; and which our beft
mezzotinto-fcrapers at prefent ufe, to
give a ftrength to particular parts; I
fpeak

speak only of a harsh, and injudicious lineal termination.

Mezzotinto excels each of the other species of prints, in its capacity of receiving the most beautiful effects of light and shade: as it can the most happily unite them, by blending them together.—Of this REMBRANDT seems to have been aware. He had probably seen some of the first mezzotintos; and admiring the effect, endeavoured to produce it in etching, by a variety of inter secting scratches.

You cannot well cast off more than an hundred good impressions from a mezzotinto plate. The rubbing of the hand soon wears it smooth: And yet by constantly repairing it, it may be made to give four or five hundred, with tolerable strength. The first impres-

sions

fions are not always the beft. They are too black and harfh. You will commonly have the beft impreffions from the fortieth to the fixtieth: the harfh edges will be foftened-down; and yet there will be fpirit and ftrength enough left.

I fhould not conclude thefe obferva-tions, without mentioning the manner of working with the *dry needle*, as it is called; a manner between etching and engraving. It is performed by cutting the copper with a fteel point, held like a pencil; and differs from etching only in the force with which you work. This method is ufed by all engravers in their fkies, and other tender parts; and fome of them carry it into ftill more general ufe.

CHAP.

CHAPTER ·III.

Characters of the most noted Masters.

MASTERS IN HISTORY. ·

ALBERT DURER, tho not the inventor, was one of the first improvers
of the art of engraving.   He was a German painter, and at the same time a
man of letters, and a philosopher.   It
may be added in his praise, that he was
an intimate friend of the great Erasmus;
who revised, it is supposed, some of the
pieces

pieces which he publifhed. He was a
man of bufinefs alfo, and for many years
the leading magiftrate of Nuremburg—
His prints, confidered as the firft efforts
of a new art, have great merit. Nay,
we may add, that it is aftonifhing to fee
a new. art, in its firft effay, carried to
fuch a length. In fome of thofe prints,
which he executed on copper, the engraving is elegant to a great degree. His
Hell-fcene particularly, which was engraved in the year 1513, is as high-finifhed a print as ever was engraved, and
as happily finifhed. The labour he has
beftowed upon it, has its full effect. In
his wooden prints too we are furprifed
to fee fo much meaning, in fo- early a
mafter; the heads fo well marked; and
every part fo well executed—This artift
feems to.have underftood the principles
of

of defign. His compofition too is often pleafing; and his drawing generally good: but he knows very little of the management of light; and ftill lefs of grace: and yet his ideas are purer, and more elegant, than we could have fuppofed from the aukward archetypes, which his country and education afforded. He was certainly a man of a very extenfive genius; and, as *Vafari* remarks, would have been an extraordinary artift; if he had had an Italian, inftead of a German education. His prints are numerous. They were much admired in his own life-time, and eagerly bought up: which put his wife, who was a teafing woman, upon urging him to fpend more time upon engraving, than he was inclined to do. He was rich, and chófe rather to praatife his art

as

as an amufement, than as a bufinefs. He died in the year 1527.

The immediate fucceffors, and imitators of ALBERT DURER, were LUCAS VAN LEIDEN, ALDGRAVE, PENS, HISBEN, and fome others of lefs note. Their works are very much in their mafter's ftyle; and were the admiration of an age which had feen nothing better. The beft of ALDGRAVE's works are two or three fmall pieces of the ftory of Lot.

GOLTZIUS flourifhed a little after the death of thefe mafters; and carried engraving to a great height. He was a native of Germany, where he learned his art; but travelling afterwards into Italy, he improved his ideas. You plainly difcover in him a mixture of the

the Flemiſh and Italian ſchools. His
forms have ſometimes a degree of elegance in them; but, in general, the
Dutch maſter prevails. GOLTZIUS is
often happy in *deſign* and *diſpoſition*; and
fails moſt in the *diſtribution of light*. But
his chief excellence lies in *execution.*
He engraves in a noble, firm, expreſſive
manner; which hath ſcarce been excelled
by any ſucceeding maſters. There is a
variety too in his execution, which is
very pleaſing. His print of the *circum-
ciſion* is one of the beſt of his works.
The ſtory is well told; the groups agreeably diſpoſed; and the execution admirable: but the figures are Dutch; and
the whole, through the want of a proper
diſtribution of ſhade, is only a glaring
maſs.

F   MULLER

MULLER engraved very much in the
ftyle of GOTZIUS; and yet in a ftill
bolder and firmer manner. We have
no where greater mafter-pieces in execution, than the works of this artift exhibit. The *baptifm of* JOHN is perhaps
the moft beautiful fpecimen of bold engraving, that is extant.

ABRAHAM BLOEMART was a Dutch
mafter alfo, and contemporary with
GOLTZIUS. We are not informed what
particular means of improvement he had;
but it is certain he defigned in a more
elegant tafte, than any of his country-
men. His figures are often graceful;
excepting only, that he gives them
fometimes an affected twift; which is
ftill more confpicuous in the fingers:
an affectation which we fometimes alfo
find

find in the prints of GOLTZIUS.—The *refurrection of* LAZARUS is one of BLOE-MART's mafter-pieces; in which are many faults, and many beauties; both very characteriftic.

While the Dutch mafters were thus carrying the art of engraving to fo great a height; it was introduced into Italy by ANDREA MANTEGNA; to whom the Italians afcribe the invention of it. The paintings of this mafter abound in noble paffages; but are formal and difagreeable. We have a fpecimen of them at Hampton-Court, in the triumph of JULIUS CÆSAR.—His prints, which are faid to have been engraved on tin plates, are tranfcripts from the fame ideas. We fee in them the chafte, correct out-line, and noble fimplicity of the Roman

fchool;

fchool: but we are to expect nothing more; not the leaft attempt towards an agreeable *whole*.—And indeed, we fhall perhaps find, in general, that the mafters of the Roman fchool were more ftudious of thofe effentials of painting, which regard the *parts*; and the Flemifh mafters, of thofe, which regard the *whole*. The former therefore drew better *figures*; the latter made better *pictures*.

MANTEGNA was fucceeded by PARMIGIANO and PALMA, both mafters of great reputation. PARMIGIANO having formed the moft accurate tafte upon a thorough ftudy of the works of RAPHAEL and MICHAEL ANGELO, publifhed many fingle figures, and fome defigns engraven on wood, which abounded with every kind of beauty; if we may form

a judga judgment of them from the few which we fometimes meet with. Whether PARMIGIANO invented the art of engraving on wood, does not certainly appear. His pretenfions to the invention of etching are lefs difputable. In this way he publifhed many flight pieces, which do him great credit. In the midft of his labours, he was interrupted by a knavifh engraver, who pilaged him of all his plates. Unable to bear the lofs, he forfwore his art, and abandoned himfelf to chymiftry.

PALMA was too much employed as a painter to have much leifure for etching. He hath left feveral prints, however, behind him; which are remarkable for the delicacy of the drawing, and the freedom of the execution. He etches

in

in a loose, but masterly manner. His prints are scarce: and indeed we seldom meet with any that deserve more than the name of sketches.

Francis Paria seems to have copied the manner of Palma with great success. But his prints are still scarcer than his master's; nor have we a sufficient number of them, to enable us to form a judgment of his merit.

But the great improver of the art of engraving on wood; and who at once carried it to a degree of perfection, which hath not since been exceeded; was Andrea Andreani, of Mantua. The works of this master are remarkable for the freedom, strength, and spirit of the execution; the elegant correctness of the

the drawing; and in general for their effect. Few prints come so near the idea of painting. They have a force, which a pointed tool upon copper cannot reach : and the wash, of which the middle tint is compofed, adds all the foftnefs of drawing. But the works of this mafter are feldom feen in perfection. They are fcarce; and when we do meet with them, it is a chance if the impreffions be good: and very much of the beauty of thefe prints depends on the goodnefs of the impreffion. For often the out-line is left hard, the middle tint being loft; and fometimes the middle tint is left without its proper termination.

Among the ancient Italian mafters, we cannot omit MARK ANTONIO ; and
AUGUSTIN

AUGUSTIN of Venice. They are both celebrated; and have handed down to us many engravings from the works of RAPHAEL: but their *antiquity*, not their *merit*, feems to have recommended them. Their execution is harfh, and formal to the laft degree: and if their prints give us any idea of the works of RAPHAEL, we may well wonder; as PICART obferves, how that mafter got his reputation.—But we cannot, perhaps, in England, form an adequate idea of thefe mafters. I have been told, their beft works are fo much valued in Italy, that they are engroffed there by the curious: that very few of them find their way into other countries; and that what we have, are, in general, but the refufe.

FREDERIC

FREDERIC BAROCCHI was born at Urbin; where the genius of RAPHAEL infpired him. In his early youth he traveled to Rome: and giving himfelf up to intenfe ftudy, he acquired a great name in painting. At his leifure hours he etched a few prints from his own defigns; which are highly finifhed, and executed with great foftnefs and delicacy. The *Salutation* is his capital performance: of which we feldom meet with any impreffions, but thofe taken from the retouched plate, which are very harfh.

ANTHONY TEMPESTA was a native of Florence, but refided chiefly at Rome; where he was employed in painting by GREGORY XIII.——His prints are very numerous: all from his own defigns.

Battles

Battles and huntings are the subjects in which he most delighted. His merit lies in expression, both in feature and in action; in the grandeur of his ideas; and in the fertility of his invention. His figures are often elegant, and graceful; and his heads marked with great spirit, and correctness. His horses, tho fleshy and ill drawn, and evidently never copied from nature; are, however, noble animals; and display an endless variety of beautiful actions— His imperfections at the same time, are very glaring. His composition is generally bad. Here and there you have a good group; seldom an agreeable whole. He had not the art of preserving his back-grounds tender; so that we are not to expect any effect of keeping.

ing. His execution is harfh; and he is totally ignorant of the diftribution of light.—But notwithftanding all his faults, fuch is his merit, that, as ftudies at leaft, his prints deferve a much higher rank in the cabinets of connoiffeurs, than they generally find: you can fcarce pick out one of them, which does not furnifh materials for an excellent com-pofition.

Augustin Carrache has left a few etchings; which are admired for the delicacy of the drawing, and the freedom of the execution. But there is great flatnefs in them, and want of ftrength. Etchings, indeed, in this ftyle are rather meant as fketches, than as finifhed prints.

Guido's

Guido's etchings, moſt of which are ſmall, are eſteemed for the ſimplicity of the deſign; the elegance and correct-neſs of the outline; and that grace, for which this maſter is remarkable. The extremities of his figures are particular-ly touched with great accuracy. But we have the ſame flatneſs in the works of Guido, which we find in thoſe of his maſter Carrache; accompanied, at the ſame time, with leſs freedom. The *parts* are finiſhed; but the *whole* ne-glected.

Cantarini copied the manner of Guido, as Paria did that of Palma; and ſo happily, that it is often difficult to diſtinguiſh the works of theſe two maſters.

Callot

CALLOT was little acquainted with any of the grand principles of painting: of compofition, and the management of light he was totally ignorant. But tho he could not make a picture, he was admirably fkilled in drawing a figure. His attitudes are generally graceful, when they are not affected; his expreffion ftrong; his drawing correct; and his execution mafterly, tho rather laboured. His *Fair* is a good epitome of his works. Confidered as a *whole*, it is a confufed jumble of ideas; but the *parts*, feparately examined, appear the work of a mafter. The fame character may be given of his moft famous work, the *Miferies of war:* in which there is more expreffion, both in action and feature, than was ever perhaps fhewn in fo fmall a compafs. And yet I know

not

not whether his *Beggars* be not the more
capital performance. In the *Miseries of
war*, he aims at compofition; in which
he rarely fucceeds: His *Beggars* are detached figures, in which lay his ftrength.
I have feen a very large work, by this
mafter, in two prints; each of them
near four feet fquare, reprefenting the
fiege of Toulon. They are rather indeed perfpective plans, than pictures.
The pains employed on them, is aftonifhing. They contain multitudes of
figures; and, in miniature, reprefent all
the humour, and all the employment of
a camp.———I fhall only add, that a vein
of drollery runs through all the defigns
of this mafter: which fometimes, when
he chufes to indulge it freely, as in the
Temptation of St. ANTHONY, difplays itfelf in a very facetious manner.

COUNT

Count Gaude contracted a friend-ship at Rome with Adam Elshamer; from whose designs he engraved a few prints. Gaude was a young nobleman upon his travels; and never practised engraving as a profession. This would call for indulgence, if his prints had less merit : but in their way, they are beautiful; tho on the whole, formal, and unpleasant. They are highly finished; and this correctness has deprived them of all freedom. Moon-lights, and torch-lights are the subjects he chuses; and his great excellence lies in preserving the effects of these different lights. His prints are generally small. I know only one, the *Flight into Egypt*, of a larger size,

SALVATOR

SALVATOR ROSA *painted* landſhip more than hiſtory; but his *prints* are chiefly hiſtorical. He was bred a painter; and perfectly underſtood his art : if we except only the *management of light,* of which he ſeems to have been ignorant. The capital landſkip of this maſter at Chiſwick is a noble picture. The contrivance, the compoſition, the diſtances, the figures, and all the parts and appendages of it are fine : but in point of light it might perhaps have been improved, if the middle ground, where the figures of the ſecond diſtance ſtand, had been thrown into ſun-ſhine. — In *deſign,* and generally in *compoſition,* SALVATOR is very great. His figures, which he drew in exquiſite taſte, are graceful, and nobly expreſſive, beautifully grouped, and varied in the moſt agreable attitudes

titudes, In the legs, it muſt be owned, he is a *manneriſt:* They are well
drawn; but all caſt in one mould.
There is a ſtiffneſs too in the backs of
his extended hands: the palms are
beautiful. But theſe are trivial criti-
ciſms.——His *manner* is ſlight; ſo as
not to admit either ſoftneſs or effect:
yet the ſimplicity and elegance of it are
wonderfully pleaſing; and bear that
ſtrong characteriſtic of a maſter's hand,
ſibi quivis ſperet idem.——One thing in
his manner of ſhading, is diſagreeable.
He will often ſhade a *face* half over with
long lines; which, in ſo ſmall and delicate an object, gives an unpleaſant ab-
ruptneſs. It is treating a face like an
egg: no diſtinction of feature is obſerved.——SALVATOR was a man of genius,
and of learning; both which he has

G

found

found frequent opportunities of difplaying in his works. His ftyle is grand; every object that he introduces is of the heroic kind; and his fubjects in general fhew an intimacy with ancient hiftory, and mythology.——A roving difpofition, to which he is faid to have given a full fcope, feems to have added a wildnefs to all his thoughts. We are told, he fpent the early part of his life in a troop of banditti: and that the rocky and defolate fcenes, in which he was accuftomed to take refuge, furnifhed him with thofe romantic ideas in landfkip, of which he is fo exceedingly fond; and in the defcription of which he fo greatly excels. His *Robbers*, as his detached figures are commonly called, are fuppofed alfo to have been taken from the life.

REM-

: REMBRANDT's excellency, as a painter, lay in colouring; which he poffeffed
in fuch perfection, that it almoft fcreens
every fault in his pictures. His prints,
deprived of this palliative, have only his
inferior qualifications to recommend
them. Thefe are expreffion, and fkill
in the management of light, execution,
and fometimes compofition. I mention
them in the order in which he feems to
have poffeffed them. His expreffion
has moft force in the character of age.
He marks as ftrongly as the hand of
time itfelf. He poffeffes too, in a great
degree, that inferior kind of expreffion,
which gives its proper, and characteriftic
touch to drapery, fur, metal, and every
object he reprefents.—His management
of light confifts chiefly in making a very ftrong contraft; which has often a

G 2   good

good effect: and yet in many of his prints, there is no effect at all: which gives us reason to think, he either had no principles; or publifhed fuch prints before his principles were afcertained.—— His execution is peculiar to himfelf. It is rough, or neat, as he meant a fketch, or a finifhed piece; but always free and mafterly. It produces its effect by ftrokes interfected in every direction; and comes nearer the idea of painting, than the execution of any other mafter.—— Never painter was more at a lofs than REMBRANDT, for an idea of that fpecies of grace, which is neceffary to fupport an elevated character. While he keeps within the fphere of his genius, and contents himfelf with low fubjects, he deferves any praife. But when he attempts beauty, or dignity, it were good-natured.

natured to fuppofe, he means only bur-
lefque and caricature. He is a ftrong
contraft to SALVATOR. The one drew
all his ideas from nature, as fhe appears
with the utmoft grace and elegance:
The other caught her in her meaneft
images; and transferred thofe images into the higheft characters. Hence SAL-
VATOR exalts banditti into heroes: REM-
BRANDT degrades patriarchs into beggars. REMBRANDT, indeed, feems to
have affected awkwardnefs. He was a
man of humour; and would laugh at
thofe artifts who ftudied the antique.
"I'll fhew you my antiques," he would
cry; and then he would carry his friends
into a room furnifhed with head-dreffes,
draperies, houfhold-ftuff, and inftru-
ments of all kinds: "Thefe, he would
"add, are worth all your antiques."—
His

His best etching is that, which goes by the name of the *hundred-guildres-print*; which is in such esteem, that I have known thirty guineas given for a good impression of it. In this all his excellencies are united: and I might add, his imperfections also. Age and wretchedness are admirably described; but the principal figure is ridiculously mean.— REMBRANDT is said to have left behind him near three hundred prints; none of which are dated before 1628; none after 1659. They were in such esteem, even in his own life time, that he is said to have retouched some of them, four or five times.

PETER TESTA studied upon a plan very different from that, either of SALVATOR, or REMBRANDT. Those mas-

ters

ters drew their ideas from nature: TES-
TA, from what he efteemed a fuperior
model—the antique. Smitten with the
love of painting, this artift travelled to
Rome in the habit of a pilgrim; defti-
tute of all the means of improvement,
but what mere genius furnifhed. He
had not even intereft to procure a re-
commendation; nor had he any ad-
drefs to fubftitute in its room. The
works of fculpture fell moft obvioufly
in his way; and to thefe he applied
himfelf with fo much induftry, copying them over, and again, that he is
faid to have gotten them all by heart.
Thus qualified, he took up the pencil.
But he foon found the fchool, in which
he had ftudied, a very infufficient one to
form a painter. He had neglected colouring; and his pictures were in no
efteem.

esteem. Disappointed and mortified, he threw aside his pallet, and applied himself to etching; in which he became a thorough proficient.——His prints have great merit; tho they are little esteemed. We are seldom, indeed, to expect a coherency of design in any of them. An enthusiastic vein runs through most of his compositions; and it is not an improbable conjecture, that his head was a little disturbed. He generally crouds into his pieces such a jumble of inconsistent ideas; that it is difficult sometimes only to guess at what he aims. He was as little acquainted with the distribution of light, as with the rules of design: and yet, notwithstanding all this, his works contain an infinite fund of entertainment. There is an exuberance of fancy in him, which,

with

with all its wildnefs, is agreeable: his
ideas are fublime and noble; his drawing elegantly correct; his heads touched with uncommon fpirit, and expreffion; his figures graceful, rather too
nearly allied to the antique; his groups
often beautiful; and his execution, in
his beft etchings, for he is fometimes
unequal to himfelf, very mafterly.*
Perhaps, no prints afford more ufeful
ftudies for a painter.——The *proceffion*
of SILENUS, if we may guefs at fo confufed a defign, may illuftrate all that
hath been faid. The *whole* is as incoherent, as the *parts* are beautiful.——This
unfortunate artift was drowned in the
Tyber; and it is left uncertain, whether
by accident or defign.

* Some of his works are etched by CÆS. TESTA.

SPANI-

Spaniolet etched a few prints in a very spirited manner. No master understood better the force of every touch. Silenus *and* Bacchus, and the *Martyrdom of St.* Bartholemew, are the best of his historical prints: and yet these are inferior to some of his caricatures, which are admirably executed.

Michael Dorigny, or Old Dorigny, as he is often called, to distinguish him from Nicholas, had the misfortune to be the son-in-law of Simon Vouet; whose works he engraved, and whose imperfections he copied. His execution is free, and he preserves the lights extremely well upon single figures: his drapery too is natural, and easy: but his drawing his below criticism; in the extremities especially. In this his master

ter miſled him. VOUET excelled in compoſition; of which we have many beautiful inſtances in DORIGNY's prints.

VILLAMENA was inferior to few engravers. If he be deficient in ſtrength and effect, there is a delicacy in his manner, which is inimitable. One of his beſt prints is, the *Deſcent from the croſs*.——But his works are ſo rare, that we can ſcarce form an adequate idea of his merit.

STEPHEN DE LA BELLA was a minute genius. His manner wants ſtrength for any larger work; but in ſmall objects it appears to advantage: there is great freedom in it, and uncommon neatneſs. His figures are touched with ſpirit; and ſometimes his compoſition is good: but

he

he feldom difcovers any fkill in the management of light; tho the defect is lefs ftriking, becaufe of the fmallnefs of his pieces. His *Pont Neuf* will give us an idea of his works. Through the bad management of the light, it makes no appearance as a *whole*; tho the compofition, if we except the modern architecture, is tolerable. But the figures are marked with great beauty; and the diftances extremely fine.——Some of his fingle heads are very elegant.

LA FAGE's works confift chiefly of fketches. The great excellency of this mafter lay in drawing; in which he was perfectly fkilled. However unfinifhed his pieces are, they difcover him to have been admirably acquainted with anatomy and proportion. There is very little

tle in him befides, that is valuable; grace, and expreffion fometimes; feldom compofition: his figures are generally either too much crowded, or too diffufe. As for light and fhade, he feems to have been totally ignorant of their effect; or he could never have fhewn fo bad a tafte, as to publifh his defigns without, at leaft, a bare expreffion of the maffes of each. Indeed, we have pofitive proof, as well as negative. Where he has attempted an effect of light, he has fhewn only how little he knew of it.——His genius chiefly difplays itfelf in the gambols of nymphs and fatyrs; in routs and revels: but there is fo much obfcenity in his works of this kind, that, altho otherwife fine, they fcarce afford an innocent amufement.——In fome of his prints, in which he has attempted the

fublimeft

fublimeft characters, he has given them
a wonderful dignity. Some of his figures of Chrift are not inferior to the
ideas of RAPHAEL: and in a flight
fketch, intitled, *Vocation de Moyfe*, the
Deity is introduced with furprizing majefty.——His beft works are flightly
etched from his drawings by ERTINGER;
who has done juftice to them.

BOLSWERT engraved the works of
RUBENS, and in a ftyle worthy of his
mafter. You fee the fame free, and
animated manner in both. It is faid
that RUBENS touched his proofs; and
it is probable: the ideas of the painter
are fo exactly transfufed into the works
of the engraver.

PONTIUS

PONTIUS too engraved the works of RUBENS; and would have appeared a greater mafter, if he had not had fuch a competitor as BOLSWERT.

SCIAMINOSSI etched a few fmall plates, of the *myfteries of the rofary*, in a mafter-ly ftyle. There is no great beauty in the compofition; but the drawing is good; tne figures are generally grace-ful; and the heads touched with great fpirit.

ROMAN LE HOOGHE is inimitable in execution. Perhaps, no mafter etches in a freer and more fpirited manner: there is a richnefs in it likewife, which we feldom meet with. His figures too are often good; but his compofition is generally faulty: it is crouded, and confufed.

confufed. He knows little of the effect
of light. There is a flutter in him too,
which hurts an eye pleafed with fimplicity. His prints are generally hiftorical. The *deluge at Coeverden* is finely
defcribed.—LE HOOGHE was much employed, by the authors of his time, in
compofing frontifpieces; fome of which
are very beautiful.

LUIKEN etches in the manner of LE
HOOGHE, but it is a lefs mafterly manner. His *hiftory of the bible* is a great
work; in which there are many good
figures, and great freedom of execution:
but poor compofition, much confufion,
and little fkill in the diftribution of
light. This mafter hath alfo etched a
book of various kinds of capital pu-
nifhment;

nifhment; amongft which there are many good prints.

Gerrard Lairesse etches in a loofe,
and unfinifhed; but free, and mafterly
manner. His light is often well diftributed; but his fhades have not fufficient
ftrength to give his pieces effect. Tho
he was a Dutch painter, you fee nothing
of the Dutchman in his works. His
compofition is generally elegant and
beautiful; efpecially where he has only
a few figures to manage. His figures
themfelves are graceful, and his expreffions ftrong.—It may be added, that his
draperies are particularly excellent.
The fimple and fublime ideas, which
appear every where in his works, acquired him the title of the *Dutch* Raphael; a title which he very well deferves.

H   Lairesse

LAIRESSE may be called an ethic painter. He commonly inculcates fome
truth either in morals, or religion; which
he illuftrates by a Latin fentence at the
bottom of his print.

CASTIGLIONE was an Italian painter
of fome eminence. He drew human
figures with grace and correctnefs: yet
he generally chofe fuch fubjects, as
would admit the introduction of animal
life; which often makes the more diftinguifhed part of his piece.——There is
a fimplicity in the defigns of this mafter, which is very beautiful. In compofition he excels greatly. Of his elegant groups we have many inftances, in
a fet of prints, etched from his paintings,
in a flight, free manner, by C. MACEE;
particularly in thofe of the *patriarchal*
journeyings.

Journeyings. He hath left us feveral of his *own* etchings alfo, which are very valuable. The fubjects, indeed, of fome of them, are odd, and fantaftic; and the compofition not equal to fome prints we have from his paintings, by other hands; but the execution is greatly fu-perior. Freedom, ftrength, and fpirit, are very eminent in them; and delicacy likewife, where he chufes to finifh high-ly; of which we have fome inftances.— One of his beft prints is, the *entering of* NOAH *into the ark.* The compofition; the diftribution of light; the fpirit and expreffion, with which the animals are touched; and the freedom of the exe-cution, are all admirable.

TIEPOLO was a diftinguifhed mafter: but by his merit; rather than the num-

ber

ber of his etchings. The work, on which his reputation is founded, is a feries of twenty plates, about nine inches long, and feven broad. The fubject of them is emblematical; but of difficult interpretation.ʳ They contain, however, a greater variety of rich, and elegant compofition; of excellent figures; and of fine old heads and characters, than I almoft any where have met with. They are very fcarce; at leaft, they have rarely fallen in my way.——I have feen a few other prints by this mafter: but none, except thefe, which I have thought excellent. He was a ftrange, whimfical man; and, perhaps, his beft pieces were thofe, in which he gave a loofe to the wildnefs of his imagination.

VANDER MUILEN has given us hiftorical reprefentations of feveral modern battles.

battles. His prints are generally large, and contain many good figures, and a-greeable groups: but they have no ef-fect, and feldom produce a *whole*. A difagreeable monotony (as the mufical people fpeak) runs through them all.

OTHO VENIUS has entirely the air of an Italian, tho of Dutch parentage. He had the honour of being the mafter of the celebrated RUBENS; who chiefly learned from him his knowledge of light and fhade. This artift publifhed a book of love-emblems; in which the cupids are engraved with great elegance. His pieces of fabulous hiftory have lefs merit.

GALESTRUZZI was an excellent artift. There is great firmnefs in his ftroke ;

great

great precifion ; and, at the fame time, great freedom. His drawing is good; his heads are well touched, and his draperies beautiful. He has etched feveral things from the antique ; fome of them, indeed, but indifferently. The beft of his works, which I have feen, is the *Story of* NIOBE, (a long, narrow print) from POLIDORE.

MELLAN was a whimfical engraver. He fhadowed entirely with parellel lines; which he winds round the mufcles of his figures, and the folds of his draperies, with great variety and beauty. His manner is foft and delicate; but void of ftrength and effect. His compofitions of courfe make no *whole*, tho his fingle figures are often elegant. His faints and ftatues are, in general, his beft pieces. There

There is great expreſſion in many of the former; and his drapery is often incomparable. One of his beſt prints is inſcribed, *Per ſe ſurgens :* and another very good one, with this ſtrange paſſage from St. AUSTIN ; *Ego evangelio non crederem, niſi me catholicæ eccleſiæ commoveret auĉto-ritas.* — His head of Chriſt, effected by a ſingle ſpiral line, is a maſterly, but whimſical performance.

OSTADE's etchings, like his pictures, are admirable repreſentations of low life. They abound in humour and expreſſion ; in which lies their merit. They have little beſides to recommend them. His compoſition is generally very indifferent; and his execution no way remarkable. Sometimes, but ſeldom, you ſee an effect of light.

CORNELIUS

' CORNELIUS BEGA etches very much in the manner of OSTADE; but with more freedom.

VAN TULDEN has nothing of the Dutch master in his defign; which feems formed upon the ftudy of the antique. It is chafte, elegant, and correct...His manner is rather firm, and diftinct; than free, and fpirited. His principal work is, *the voyage of* ULYSSES, *in fifty-eight plates*; in which we have a great variety of elegant attitudes, excellent characters of heads, good drawing; and tho not much effect, yet often good grouping. His drapery is heavy.

JOSEPH PARROCELLE painted battles for LEWIS XIV. He etched alfo feveral of of his own defigns. The beft of his works are eight fmall battles, which are very fcarce. Four of thefe are of a fize larger than the reft; of which, the *battle,* and *ftripping the flain,* are very fine. Of the four fmaller, that entitled *vefper* is the beft.—His manner is rough; free, and mafterly; and his knowledge of the effect of light confiderable.— His greateft undertaking was, the *Life of Chrift,* in a feries of plates: but it is a hafty and incorrect work. Moft of the prints are mere fketches; and many of them, even in that light, are bad; tho the freedom of the manner is pleafing in the worft of them. The beft plates are the 14th, 17th, 19th, 22d, 28th, 39th, 41ft, 42d, and 43d.

V. Lt

V. LE FEBRE etched many defigns from TITIAN and JULIO ROMANO, in a very miferable manner. His drawing is bad; his drapery frittered; his lights ill-preferved; and his execution dif- gufting: and yet we find his works in capital collections.

BELLANGE's prints are highly finifh- ed, and his execution is not amifs. His figures alfo have fomething in them, which looks like grace; and his light is tolerably well maffed. But his heads are ill fet on; his extremities incorrect- ly touched; his figures badly propor- tioned; and, in fhort, his drawing in general very bad.

CLAUDE GILLOT was a French pain- ter: but finding himfelf rivalled, he laid
afide

aſide his pencil, and employed himſelf
entirely in etching. His common ſub-
jects are *dances* and *revels* ; adorned with
ſatyrs, nymphs, and fauns. By giving
his ſylvans a peculiar caſt of eye, he has
introduced a new kind of character.
The invention, and fancy of this maſter are very pleaſing ; and his compoſition is often good. His manner is
ſlight ; which is the beſt apology for his
bad drawing.

WATTEAU has great defects ; and, it
muſt be owned, great merit. He a-
bounds in all that flutter, and affecta-
tion, which is ſo diſagreeable in the ge-
nerality of French painters. But, at
the ſame time, we acknowledge, he
draws well ; gives grace and delicacy
to his figures ; and produces often a
beautiful

beautiful effect of light. I fpeak, chiefly of fuch of his works, as have been engraved by others.—He etched a few flight plates himfelf, with great freedom and elegance. The beft of them are contained in a fmall book of figures, in various dreffes and atti-tudes.

CORNELIUS SCHUT excels chiefly in execution; fometimes in compofition; but he knows nothing of grace; and has, upon the whole, but little merit.

WILLIAM BAUR etches with great fpirit. His largeft works are in the hiftorical way. He has given us many of the fieges, and battles, which wafted Flanders in the fixteenth contury. They *may* be exact, and probably they *are*; but

but they are rather plans than pictures; and have little to recommend them but hiftoric truth, and the freedom of the execution. BAUR's beft prints are, fome characters he has given us of different nations; in which the peculiarities of each are very well obferved. His OVID is a poor performance.

COYPEL hath left us a few prints of his own etching; the principal of which is, an *Ecce homo*, touched with great fpirit. Several of his own defigns he etched himfelf; and afterwards put into the hands of engravers to finifh. It is probable he overlooked the work: but we fhould certainly have had better prints, if we had received them pure from his own needle. What they had loft in

force,

force; would have been amply made up in fpirit.

PICART was one of the moft ingenious of the French engravers. His *imitations* are among the moft entertaining of his works. The cry, in his day, ran wholly in favour of antiquity: " Nó modern mafters were worth looking at." PICART, piqued at fuch prejudice, etched feveral pieces in imitation of ancient mafters; and fo happily, that he almoft out-did, in their own excellencies, the artifts whom he copied. Thefe prints were much admired, as the works of GUIDO, REMBRANDT, and others. Having had his joke, he publifhed them under the title of *Impoftures innocentes.*—PICART's own manner is highly finifhed; yet, at the fame time, rich, bold, and fpirited.

rited: his prints are generally fmall; and moft of them from the defigns of others. One of the beft is from that beautiful compofition of POUSSIN, in which *Truth is delivered by Time, from Envy.*

ARTHUR POND, our countryman, fucceeded admirably in this method of imitation; in which he hath etched feveral very valuable prints; particularly two oval landfkips after SALVATOR—a monkey in red chalk after CARRACHE —two or three ruins after PANINI, and fome others equally excellent.

But this method of imitation hath been moft fuccefsfully practifed by *Count* CAYLUS, an ingenious French nobleman; whofe works, in this way, are very voluminous. He hath ranfacked the French king's king's cabinet; and hath scarce left a master of any note, from whose drawings he hath not given us an excellent specimen. Insomuch, that if we had nothing remaining of those masters, but *Count* CAYLUS's works; we should not want a very sufficient idea of them. So versatile is his genius, that with the same ease he presents us with an elegant outline from RAPHAEL, a rough sketch from REMBRANDT, and a delicate portrait from VANDYKE.

LE CLERC was an excellent engraver; but chiefly in the petit style. He immortalized ALEXANDER, and LEWIS XIV. in miniature. His genius seldom exceeds the dimensions of six inches. Within those limits he can draw up twenty thousand men with great dexteri-

ty

ty. No artist except CALLOT and DEL-
LA BELLA, could touch a small figure
with so much spirit. He seems to have
imitated CALLOT's manner; but his
stroke is neither so firm, nor so masterly.

PETER BARTOLI etched with freedom; tho his manner is not agreeable.
His capital work is LANFRANK's gallery.

JAC. FREII is an admirable engraver.
He unites, in a great degree, strength,
and softness; and comes as near the
force of painting, as an engraver can
well do. He has given us the strongest
ideas of the works of several of the most
eminent masters. He preserves the
drawing, and expression of his original;
and often, perhaps, improves the effect.

I   There

There is a richnefs too in his manner, which is very pleafing. You fee him in perfection, in a noble print from C. MA-RATTE, intitled, *In .confpectu angelorum, pfallam tibi.*

R. V. AUDEN AERD copied many things from C. MARATTE, and other mafters; in a ftyle indeed very inferior to JAC FREII, (whofe rich execution he could not reach) but yet with fome elegance. His manner is fmooth, and finifhed; but without effect. His drawing is good, but his lights are frittered.

S. GRIBELIN is a careful, and laborious engraver; of no extenfive genius; but painfully exact. His works are chiefly fmall; the principal of which are his copies from the Banqueting-Houfe

at

at Whitehall; and from the Cartoons.
His manner is formal; yet he has contrived to preferve the fpirit of his original. We have no copies of the Cartoons
fo good as his. It is a pity he did not
engrave them on a larger fcale.

Le Bas etches in a clear, diftinct,
free manner; and has done great honour
to the works of Teniers, Woverman,
and Berghem; from whom he chiefly
copied. The beft of his works are after Berghem.

Bischop's etching has fomething very pleafing in it. It is loofe, and free;
and yet has ftrength, and richnefs. Many of his ftatues are good figures: the
drawing is fometimes incorrect; but the
execution is always beautiful. Many of

I 2   the

the plates of his drawing-book are good.
His greateſt ſingle work, is the repreſentation of JOSEPH *in Egypt*; in which
there are many faults, both in the drawing and effect; ſome of which are
chargeable upon himſelf, and others upon the artiſt from whom he copied; but
upon the whole, it is a pleaſing print.

FRANCIS PERRIER was the debauched
ſon of a goldſmith in Franchecompte.
His indiſcretions forcing him from
home, his inclinations led him to Italy.
His manner of travelling thither was
whimſical. He joined himſelf to a
blind beggar, whom he agreed to lead
for half his alms. At Rome, he applied to painting; and made a much
greater proficiency than could have been
expected from his diſſipated life. He
pub-

published a large collection of ftatues and other antiquities; which are etched in a very mafterly manner. The drawing is often incorrect ; but the attitudes are well chofen, and the execution fpirited. Many of them feem to have been done haftily; but there are marks of genius in them all.

MAROT, architect to K. WILLIAM, hath etched fome ftatues likewife, in a very mafterly manner. Indeed all his works are admirably executed; but they confift chiefly of ornaments in the way of his profeffion.

FRAN. ROETTIERS etches in a very bold manner, and with a good deal of fpirit; but there is a harfhnefs in his outline, which is difagreeable; tho the

lefs

lefs fo, as his drawing is generally good. Few artifts manage a crowd better; or give it more effect by a proper diftribution of light. Of this management we have fome judicious inftances in his two capital prints, the *Affumption of the crofs,* and the *Crucifixion.*

NICHOLAS DORIGNY was bred a lawyer: but not fucceeding at the bar, he ftudied painting; and afterwards applied to engraving. His capital work is, the *Transfiguration*; which Mr. ADDISON calls the nobleft print in the world. It is unqueftionably a noble work; but DORIGNY feems to have exhaufted his genius upon it: for he did nothing afterwards worth preferving. His Cartoons are very poor. He engraved them in his old age; and was obliged to employ affiftants, who did not anfwer his expectation.

MASTERS

Among the masters in portrait, Rem-brandt takes the lead. His heads are admirable copies from nature; and per-haps the best of his works. There is in-finite expreſſion in them, and character.

Van Uliet followed Rembrandt's manner; which he hath in many things excelled. Some of his heads are ex-ceedingly beautiful. The force which he gives to every feature, the roundneſs of the muſcle, the ſpirit of the execu-tion, the ſtrength of the character, and the effect of the whole, are all admira-ble.

J. Leivens

J. Lievens etches in the fame ftyle. His heads are executed with great fpirit; and deferve a place in any collection of prints; tho they are certainly inferior to Uliet's.—Uliet, and Lievens etched fome hiftorical prints; particularly the latter, whofe *Lazarus*, after Rembrandt, is a noble work; but their portraits are their beft prints.

Among the imitators of Rembrandt, we fhould not forget our countryman Worlidge; who has very ingenioufly followed the manner of that mafter; and fometimes improved upon him. No man underftood the drawing of an head better.—His fmall prints alfo, from antique gems, are neat, and mafterly.

Many

Many of Van Dyke's etchings do him great credit. They are chiefly to be found in a collection of the portraits of eminent artifts, which Van Dyke was at the expence of getting engraved. They are done flightly; but bear the character of a mafter. Luke Voster-man is one of the beft. It is probable Van Dyke made the drawings for moft of them: his manner is confpicuous in them all.——A very finifhed etching of an *Ecce homo,* paffes under the name of this mafter. It is a good print upon the whole; but not equal to what we might have expected.

We have a few prints of Sir Peter Lely's etching likewife; but there is nothing in them that is extraordinary.

R. White

R. WHITE was the principal engraver of portraits, in CHARLES the second's reign; but his works are miserable performances. They are said to be good likenesses; and they may be so; but they are wretched prints.

BECKET and SIMONS are names which scarce deserve to be mentioned. They were in their time, mezzotinto-scrapers of note, only because there were no others.

WHITE, the mezzotinto scraper, son of the engraver, was an artist of great merit. He copied after Sir GODFREY KNELLER; whom he teased so much with his proofs, that it is said Sir GODFREY forbad him his house. His mezzotintos are very beautiful. BAPTISTE,

WING

Wing, Sturges, and Hooper are all
admirable prints. He himfelf ufed to
fay, that old and young Parr were the
beft portraits he ever fcraped. His
manner was peculiar, at the time he
ufed it: tho it hath fince been adopted
by other mafters. He firft etched his
plate, and then fcraped it. Hence his
prints preferve a fpirit to the laft, which
few mezzotintos do.

Smith was the pupil of Becket; but
he foon excelled his mafter. He was
efteemed the beft mezzotinto fcraper of
his time; though, perhaps, inferior to
White. He hath left a very numerous colleftion of portraits: fo numerous, that they are often bound in two
large folios. He copied chiefly from
Sir Godfrey; and is faid to have had an
apart-

apartment in his houfe.—LORD SOMERS
was fo fond of the works of this mafter; that he feldom travelled, without
carrying them with him in the feat of
his coach.—Some of his beft prints are
two holy families, ANTHONY LEIGH,
MARY MAGDALENE, SCALKEN, an half-
length of Lady ELIZABETH CROMWELL,
the Duke of SCHOMBERG on horfe-back,
the countefs of SALISBURY, GIBBON the
ftatuary, and a very fine hawking piece
from WYKE.——After all, it muft be
owned, that the beft of thefe mezzotintos are inferior to what we have feen
done by the mafters of the prefent age.

MELLAN's portaits are the moft indifferent of his works. They want ftrength,
fpirit, and effeɛt.

PITTERI

PITTERI hath lately publiſhed a ſet
of heads, from PIAZZETA, in the ſtyle
of MELLAN; but in a much finer taſte,
both as to the compoſition, and the
manner. Tho, like MELLAN, he never croſſes his ſtroke; yet he has contrived to give his heads more force and
ſpirit.

J. MORIN's heads are engraved in a
very peculiar manner. They are ſtip-
pled with a graver, after the manner
of mezzotinto; and have a good effect.
They have force; and, at the ſame
time, ſoftneſs. Few portraits, upon
the whole, are better. GUIDO BENTI-
VOLIUS from VANDYKE is one of the
beſt.

J. LUTMA's

J. Lutma's heads are executed in
the fame way: we are told, with a
chifel and mallet. They are inferior
to Morin's; but are not without merit.

Edm. Marmion etched a few portraits in the manner of Vandyke, and
probably from him; in which there is
eafe and freedom. He has put his name
only to one of them.

Wolfang, a German engraver, managed his tools with foftnefs, and delicacy; at the fame time preferving a confiderable degree of fpirit. But his works
are fcarce. I make thefe remarks indeed, from a fingle head, that of Huet,
bifhop of Auranches; which is the only
work of his, that I have feen.

Drevet's

DREVET's portraits are neat and elegant; but laboured to the laft degree. They are copied from RIGAUD, and other French mafters; and abound in all that flutter, and licentious drapery, fo oppofite to the fimple and chafte ideas of true tafte. DREVET chiefly excels in copying RIGAUD's frippery; lace, filk, fur, velvet, and other ornamental parts of drefs,

RICHARDSON hath left us feveral heads, which he etched for Mr. POPE, and others of his friends. They are flight, but fhew the fpirit of a mafter. Mr. POPE's profile is the beft.

VERTUE was a good antiquarian, and a worthy man, but no artift. He copied with painful exactnefs; in a dry, difagreeable

difagreeable manner; without force, or freedom. In his whole collection of heads, we can fcarce pick out half a dozen, which are good.

Such an artift in mezzotinto, was FABER. He has publifhed nothing extremely bad; and yet few things worth collecting. *Mrs.* COLLIER is one of his beft prints; and a very good one. She is leaning againft a pillar; on the bafe of which is engraved the ftory of the golden apple.

HOUBRAKEN is a genius; and has given us, in his collection of Englifh portraits, fome pieces of engraving at leaft equal to any thing of the kind. Such are his heads of HAMBDEN, SCHOMBERG, the earl of BEDFORD, the duke

duke of RICHMOND particularly, and
fome others. At the fame time we muft
own, that he has intermixed among his
works, a great number of bad prints. In
his beft, there is a wonderful union of
foftnefs, and freedom. A more elegant and flowing line no artift ever employed.

Our countryman FRY has left behind
him a few very beautiful heads in mezzotinto. They are all copied from nature; have great foftnefs, and fpirit;
but want ftrength. Mezzotinto is not
adapted to works fo large, as the heads
he has publifhed.

K   MASTERS

MASTERS IN ANIMAL LIFE.

BERGHEM has a genius truly paftoral; and brings before us the moft agreeable fcenes of rural life. The fimplicity of Arcadian manners is no where better defcribed than in his works. We have a large collection of prints from his defigns; many etched by himfelf, and many by other mafters. Thofe by himfelf are flight, but mafterly. His execution is inimitable. His cattle, which are always the diftinguifhed part of his pieces, are well drawn, admirably characterized, and generally well grouped. Few painters excelled more in compofition than BERGHEM; and yet we have more beautiful inftances of it

in

in the prints etched from him by others, than in thofe by himfelf. Among his own etchings a few fmall plates of fheep, and goats are exceedingly valued.

J. VISSCHER never appears to more advantage, than when he copies BERG-HEM. His excellent drawing, and the freedom of his execution, give a great value to his prints; which have more the air of originals, than of copies. He is a mafter both in etching, and engraving. His flighteft etchings, tho copies only, are the works of a mafter; and when he touches with a graver, he knows how to add ftrength and firm-nefs, without deftroying freedom and fpirit. He might be faid to have done all things well, if he had not failed in the diftribution of light: it is more

than

than probable, he has not attended to the effect of it, in many of the paintings which he has copied.

DANKER DANKERTS is another ex_cellent copyift from BERGHEM. Every thing, that has been faid of VISSCHER, may be faid of him; and perhaps ftill in a ftronger manner.—Like VISSCHER too he fails in the management of his lights.

HONDIUS, a native of Rotterdam, paffed the greater part of his life in England. He painted animals chiefly; was free in his manner; extravagant in his colouring; incorrect in his draw-ing; ignorant of the effect of light; but great in expreffion. His prints there-fore are better than his pictures. They

poffefs

poffefs his chief excellency, with fewer
of his defects. They are executed with
great fpirit; and afford fuch ftrong inftances of animal fury, as we meet with
no where, but in nature itfelf. His
bunted wolf is an admirable print.

Du Jardin underftood the anatomy
of domeftic animals perhaps better than
any other mafter. His drawing is admirably correct; and yet the freedom of
the mafter is preferved. He copied nature ftrictly, tho not fervilely; and has
given us not only the form, but the characteriftic peculiarities, of each animal.
He never, indeed, like Hondius, ani-
mates his creation with the violence of
favage fury. His genius takes a milder
turn. All is quietnefs, and repofe. His
dogs, after their exercife, are ftretch-
ed

ed at their eafe; and the langour of a
meridian fun prevails commonly through
all his pieces. His compofition is
beautiful; and his execution, tho neat,
is fpirited. — His works, when bound
together, make a volume of about 50
leaves; among which there is fcarce
one bad print.

RUBENS's huntings are undoubtedly
fuperior upon the whole, to any thing
of the kind we have. There is more
invention in them, and a grander ftyle
of compofition, than we find any where
elfe. I clafs them under his name, becaufe they are engraved by feveral mafters. But all their engravings are poor.
They refemble the paintings they are
copied from, as a fhadow does the object which projects it. There is fomething

thing of the *shape*; but all the *finishing* is loft. And indeed there is no doubt, but the awkwardneffes, the patch-work, and the grotefque characters, which every where appear in thofe prints, are in the originals bold fore-fhortnings, grand effects of light, and noble inftances of expreffion.—But it is as difficult to copy the flights of RUBENS, as to tranflate thofe of PINDAR. The fpirit of each mafter evaporates in the procefs.

WOVERMAN's compofition is generally crouded with little ornaments. There is no fimplicity in his works. He wanted a chafte judgment to correct his exuberance.—VISSCHER was the firft, who engraved prints from this artift. He chofe only a few good defigns; and

and executed them masterly.—Mor-
reau undertook him next, and hath
publifhed a large collection. He
hath finifhed them highly; but with
more foftnefs than fpirit. His prints
however have a neat appearance, and
exhibit a variety of pleafing reprefentations; cavalcades, marches, huntings, and encampments.

Rosa of Tivoli etched in a very finifhed manner. No one out-did him
in compofition, and execution: He is
very fkilful too in the management of
light. His defigns are all paftoral; and
yet there is often a mixture of the heroic
ftyle in his compofition, which is very
pleafing. His prints are fcarce; and,
were they not fo, would be valuable.

Stephen.

STEPHEN DE LA BELLA may be mentioned among the mafters in animal
life ; tho few of his works in this way
deferve any other praife, than what a-
rifes from the elegance of the execution.
In general, his animals are neither
well drawn, nor juftly charaƈterized.
The beft of his works in animal life are
fome heads of camels and dromedaries.

ANTHONY TEMPESTA hath etched
feveral plates of fingle horfes; and of
huntings. He hath given great expreffion to his animals; but his compofition is more than ordinarily bad in
thefe prints: nor is there in any of them
the leaft effeƈt of light.

J. FYT hath-etched a few animals;
in which you difcover the drawing, and
fome-

fomething of that inimitable ftrength
and fpirit, with which he painted. But
he has only done a few detached things
in this way; nothing to fhew his fkill in
compofition, and the management of
light, both which he well underftood.

· In curious collections we meet with a
few of CUYP's etchings. The *pictures*
of this mafter excel in colouring, compofition, drawing, and the expreffion of
character. His *prints* have all thefe excellencies, except the firft.

PETER DE LAER hath left us feveral
fmall etchings of horfes, and other
animals, well characterized, and executed in a bold and mafterly manner.
Some of them are fingle figures; but
when he compofes, his compofition is
generally

generally good, and his diftribution of light feldom much amifs; often very pleafing: his drawing too is commonly good.

PETER STOOP came from Lifbon with queen Catharine; and was admired in England, till WYCK's fuperior excellence in painting eclipfed him. He hath etched a book of horfes, which are very much valued; as there is in general, accuracy in the drawing, nature in the characters, and fpirit in the execution.

REMBRANDT's lions, which are etched in his ufual ftyle, are worthy the notice of a connoiffeur.

BLOTELING's

BLOTELING's lions are highly finifhed; but with more neatnefs than fpirit.

PAUL POTTER etched feveral plates
of cows and horfes in a, mafterly manner. His manner, indeed, is better
than his drawing; which, in his fheep
efpecially, is but very indifferent: neither does he characterize them with any
accuracy.

BARLOW's etchings are numerous.
His illuftration of Efop is his greateft
work. There is fomething pleafing in
the compofition and manner of this
mafter, tho neither is excellent. His
drawing too is very indifferent; nor
does he characterize any animal juftly.

His

His birds in general are better than his beafts.

FLAMEN has etched feveral plates of birds and fifhes: the former are bad; the latter better than any thing of the kind we have.

HOLLAR has given us feveral plates in animal life; which ought the rather to be taken notice of, as they are, per-haps, among the beft of his works. Two or three fmall plates of domeftic fowls, ducks, wood-cocks, and other game, are very well. His fhells, and butterflies are beautiful.

I fhall clofe this account with RIDIN-GER, who is one of the greateft mafters in animal life. He is ftill living; but

as

as he is fo capital in this way, he muſt not be omitted. This artiſt has mark-ed the characters of animals, eſpecially of the more favage kind, with great expreſſion. His works may be conſi-dered as natural hiſtory. He carries us into the foreſt among bears, and ty-gers; and, with the exactneſs of a na-turaliſt, deſcribes their forms, haunts, and manner of living.——His compo-ſition is generally beautiful; ſo that he commonly produces an agreeable whole. His landſkip too is picturesque and ro-mantic; and well adapted to the fubjects he treats.—On the other hand, his man-ner is laboured, and wants freedom. His human figures are feldom drawn with taſte. His horſes are ill-characterized, and worſe drawn; and, indeed, his draw-ing, in general, is but flovenly.—The

prints

prints of this master are often real history; and reprefent the portraits of particular animals, which had been taken
in hunting. We have fometimes too,
the ftory of the chace in high-dutch,
at the bottom of the print. The idea
of hiftorical truth adds a relifh to the
entertainment; and we furvey the animal with new pleafure, which has given
diverfion to a German prince for nine
hours together.——The productions of
RIDINGER are very numerous; and the
greater part of them good. His huntings in general, and different methods
of catching animals, are the leaft picturefque of any of his works. But he
meant them rather as didactic prints,
than as pictures. Many of his fables
are beautiful; particularly the 3d, the
7th, the 8th, and the 10th. I cannot
                                    forbear

forbear adding a particular encomium, upon a book of the heads of wolves and foxes.—His moſt capital prints are two large uprights; one reprefenting bears devouring a deer; the other, wild-boars repofing in a foreſt.

MASTERS

Sadler's landfcapes have fome merit in compofition : they are picturefque and romantic; but the manner is dry and difagreeable; the light ill-diftributed; the diftances ill-kept; and the figures bad.—There were three engravers of this name; but none of them eminent. John engraved a fet of prints for the bible; and many other fmall plates in the hiftorical way: in which we fometimes find a graceful figure, and tolerable drawing; but, on the whole, no great merit. Egidius was the engraver of landfcapes; and is the perfon here criticifed. Ralph chiefly copied the defigns of Bassan; and en-

L graved

graved in the dry difagreeable manner of his brother.

REMBRANDT's landfcapes have very little to recommend them, befides their effect; which is often furprifing. One of the moft admired of them goes under the name of *The three trees.*

GASPER POUSSIN etched a few landfcapes in a very loofe, but mafterly manner. It is a pity we have not more of his works.

ABRAHAM BLOEMART underftood the beauty of compofition, as well in landfcape, as in hiftory. But his prints have little force, through the want of a proper diftribution of light. Neither is there much freedom in the execution.

HOLLAR

Hollar gives us views of particular places ; which he copies with great truth, unadorned as he found them. If we are satisfied with exact reprefentations, we have them no where better than in Hollar's works: but we are not to expect pictures. Hollar was an antiquarian, and a draughtfman ; but feems to have been little acquainted with the principles of painting. Stiffnefs is his characteriftic, and a painful exactnefs, void of tafte. His larger views are mere plans. In his fmaller, fometimes an effect is produced : But in general, we confider him as a repofitory of curiofities, a record of antiquated dreffes, abolifhed ceremonies, and edifices now in ruins.

L 2   Stephen

STEPHEN DE LA BELLA's landſcapes have little to recommend them, beſides their neatneſs, and keeping. His com-poſition is ſeldom good; and the foliage of his trees reſembles bits of ſpunge. I ſpeak chiefly of his larger works; for which his manner is not calculated. His neatneſs qualifies him better for miniature.

BOLSWERT's landſcapes after REUBENs are executed in a grand ſtyle. Such a painter, and ſuch an engraver, could not fail of producing ſomething great. There is little variety in them: nor any of the more minute beauties ariſing from con-traſts, catching lights, and ſuch little elegancies; but every thing is ſimple, and great. The print, which goes by the name of *The waggon,* is particularly, and

and defervedly admired. Of thefe prints
you generally meet with good impreffions; as the plates are engraved with
great ftrength.

Neulant hath etched a fmall book
of the ruins of Rome ; in which there is
great fimplicity, and fome fkill in compofition, and the diftribution of light :
but the execution is harfh and difagreeable.

We have a few landfcapes by an earl
of *Sunderland*, in an elegant, loofe manner. One of them, in which a Spaniard
is ftanding on the fore-ground, is marked *G. & J. fculpferunt:* another *J. G.*

Waterlo is a name beyond any other
in landfcape. His fubjects are perfectly

ly rural. Simplicity is their characteriftic. We find no great variety in them,
nor ftretch of fancy. He felects a few
humble objects. A coppice, a corner
of a foreft, a winding road, or a ftrag-
ling village is generally the extent of
his view: nor does he always introduce
an offfkip. His compofition is generally good, and his light often well diftributed; but his chief merit lies in execution; in which he is a confummate
mafter. Every object that he touches,
has the character of nature: but he particularly excels in the foliage of trees.
—It is a difficult matter to meet with
the works of this mafter in perfection;
the original plates are all retouched, and
greatly injured.

SWANEVELT

SWANEVELT painted landfcape at
Rome; where he obta'ned the name of
the hermit, from his folitary walks among
the ruins of TIVOLI, and FRESCATI. He
etched in the manner of WATERLO;
but with lefs freedom. His trees, in
particular, will bear no comparifon with
thofe of that mafter. But if he fell fhort
of WATERLO in the freedom of execution, he went greatly beyond him in the
dignity of defign. WATERLO faw nature with a Dutchman's eye. If we except two or three of his pieces, he never went beyond the plain fimplicity of
a Flemifh landfcape. SWANEVELT's ideas
were of a nobler caft. SWANEVLET had
trodden claffic ground; and had warm-
ed his imagination with the grandeur
and variety of Italian views, every where
ornamented with the fplendid ruins of
Roman

Roman architecture. His compofition is often good; and his lights judicioufly fpread. In his execution, we plainly dif-cover two manners: whether a number of his plates have been retouched by fome judicious hand; or whether he himfelf altered his manner in the diffe-rent periods of his life.

JAMES ROUSSEAU, the difciple of SWANEVELT, was a French proteftant; and fled into England from the perfecu-tion of Lewis XIV. Here he was pa-tronized by the duke of MONTAGUE; whofe palace, now the *Britifh Mufeum*, he contributed to adorn with his paint-ings; fome of which are good. The few etchings he hath left are beautiful. He underftood compofition, and the diftribution of light; and there is a fine tafte

tafte in his landfcapes ; if we except perhaps only that his horizon is often taken
too high. Neither can his perfpective,
at all times, bear a critical examination ; and what is worfe, it is often pe-
dantically introduced. His figures are
good in themfelves, and generally well
placed.—His manner is rather dry and
formal.—Rousseau, it may be added,
was an excellent man. Having efcaped
the rage of perfecution himfelf, he made
it his ftudy to leffen the fufferings of his
diftreffed brethren ; by diftributing a-
mong them the greateft part of his gains.
Such an anecdote, in the life of a painter, fhould not be omitted, even in fo
fhort a review as this.

We now and then meet with an etching by Ruysdale ; but I never faw any,
that was not exceedingly flight.

J. Lutma

J. Lutma hath etched a few small landscapes in a masterly manner; which discover some skill in composition, and the management of light.

Israel Sylvestre has given us small views (some indeed of a larger size) of most of the capital ruins, churches, bridges and castles, in France and Italy. They are exceedingly neat, and touched with great spirit. This master can give beauty even to the outlines of a modern building; and what is more, he gives it without injuring the truth: insomuch that I have seen a gentleman just come from his travels, pick out many of Sylvestre's views, one by one, (tho he had never seen them before) merely from his acquaintance with the buildings. To his praise it may be farther

ther added, that in general he forms his
view into an agreeable whole ; and if
his light is not always well diftributed, there are fo many beauties in his
execution, that the eye cannot find
fault. His works are very numerous,
and few of them are bad. In trees he
excels leaft.

The etchings of CLAUDE LORRAIN
are below his character. His execution
is bad : there is a dirtinefs in it, which
is difgufting : his trees are heavy; his
lights feldom well-maffed; and his diftances only fometimes obferved.——
The truth is, CLAUDE's talents lay upon
his pallet; and he could do nothing
without it.——His *Via facra* is one of
his beft prints. The trees and ruins on
the left, are beautifully touched; and
the

the whole (tho a formal whole) would
have been pleafing, if the fore-ground
had been in fhadow.

PERELLE has great merit. His fancy is fruitful; and fupplies him with a
richnefs, and variety in his views, which
nature feldom exhibits. It is indeed
too exuberant; for he often confounds
the eye with too great a luxuriancy.
His manner is his own; and it is hard to
fay, whether it excels moft in richnefs,
ftrength, elegance, or freedom. His
trees are particularly beautiful; the foliage is loofe, and the ramification eafy.
And yet it muft be confeffed, that PE-
RELLE is rather a mannerift, than a co-
pier of nature. His views are all ideal;
his trees are of one family; and his light,
tho generally well diftributed, is fometimes

times affected: it is introduced as a
spot; and is not properly melted into
the neighbouring fhade by a middle
tint. Catching lights, ufed fparingly,
are beautiful: PERELLE affects them.——
Thefe remarks are made principally on
the works of *old* PERELLE: For there
were three engravers of this name; the
grand-father, the father, and the fon.
They all engraved in the fame ftyle; but
the juniors, inftead of improving the
family tafte, degenerated. The grand-
father is the beft, and the grandfon the
worft.

VANDER CABEL feems to have been a
carelefs artift; and difcovers great flo-
venlinefs in many of his works: but in
thofe which he has ftudied, and carefully executed, there is great beauty.
His

His manner is loose and masterly. It wants effect; but abounds in freedom. His trees are often particularly well managed; and his small pieces, in general, are the best of his works.

In WEIROTTER we see great neatness, and high finishing; but often at the expence of spirit and effect. He seems to have understood best the management of trees; to which he always gives a beautiful loosenefs.——There is great effect in a small moon-light by this master: the whole is in dark shade, except three figures on the fore-ground.

OVERBECK etched a book of Roman ruins; which are in general good. They are pretty large, and highly finished. His manner is free, his light often well
distributed,

diſtributed, and his compoſition agreeable.

GENOEL's landſcapes are rather free
ſketches, than finiſhed prints. In that
light they are beautiful. No effect is
aimed at: but the free manner in which
they are touched, is pleaſing; and the
compoſition is in general good, tho often crowded.

BOTH's taſte in landſcape is elegant.
His ideas are grand; his compoſition
beautiful; and his execution rich and
maſterly in a high degree. His light
is not always well diſtributed ; but his
figures are excellent. We regret that
we have not more of his works; for they
are certainly, upon the whole, among
the beſt landſcapes we have.

MARCO

Marco Ricci's works, which are numerous, have little merit. His human figures indeed are good, and his trees tolerable; but he produces no effect, his manner is difgufting, his cattle ill-drawn, and his diftances ill-preferved.

Le Veau's landfcapes are highly finifhed: they are engraved with great foftnefs, elegance, and fpirit. The keeping of this mafter is particularly well obferved. His fubjects too are well-chofen; and his prints indeed, in general, make beautiful furniture.

Zuingo engraves in a manner very like Le Veau; but not quite fo elegantly.

Zeeman

ZEEMAN was a Dutch painter; and
excelled in fea-coafts, beaches, and diftant land; which he commonly adorned
with fkiffs, and fifhing-boats. His execution is neat, and his diftances well
kept: but he knows nothing of the diftribution of light. His figures too are
good, and his fkiffs admirable. In his
fea-pieces he introduces larger veffels ;
but his prints in this ftyle are commonly awkward, and difagreeable.

VANDIEST left behind him a few
rough fketches, which are executed with
great freedom.

GOUPY very happily caught the manner of SALVATOR; and in fome things
excelled him. There is a richnefs in
his execution, and a fpirit in his trees,

M   which

which SALVATOR wants. But his figures are bad. Very grofs inftances,
not only of indelicacy of out-line, but
even of bad drawing, may be found in
his print of PORSENNA, and in that of
DIANA. Landfcape is his fort; and his
beft prints are thofe, which go under
the titles of the *Latrones*, the *Augurs*,
Tobit, *Hagar*, and its companion.

PIRANESI has given us a larger collection of Roman antiquities, than any
other mafter; and has added to his ruins a great variety of modern buildings.
The critics fay, he has trufted too much
to his eye; and that his proportions and
perfpective are often faulty. He feems
to be a rapid genius; and we are told,
the drawings, which he takes upon the
fpot, are as flight and rough as poffible:
the

the reft he makes out by memory and invention. From fo voluminous an artift, indeed we cannot expect much correctnefs: his works complete, fell at leaft for fifty pounds.——But the great excellence of this artift lies in execution; of which he is a confummate mafter. His ftroke is firm, free, and bold, beyound expreffion; and his manner admirably culculated to produce a grand, and rich effect. But the effects he produces are rarely feen, except in fingle objects. A defaced capital, a ruined wall, or broken fluting, he touches with great foftnefs, and fpirit. He expreffes even the ftains of weather-beaten marble: and thofe of his prints, in which he has an opportunity of difplaying expreffion in this way, are generally the beft. His ftroke has much the appearance of

etching;

etching; but I have been informed that it is chiefly engraved, and that he makes great ufe of the dry needle.—His faults are many. His horizon is often taken too high; his views are frequently ill-chofen; his objects crowded; and his forms ill-fhaped. Of the diftribution of light he has little knowledge. Now and then we meet with an effect of it; which makes us only lament, that in fuch mafterly performances it is found fo feldom. His figures are bad: they are ill-drawn, and the drapery hangs in tatters. It is the more unhappy, as his prints are populous. His trees are in a paltry ftyle; and his fkies hard, and frittered.

Our celebrated countryman HOGARTH cannot properly be omitted in a catalogue of engravers; and yet he ranks

in

in none of the foregoing claffes. With
this apology I fhall introduce him here.

The works of this mafter abound in
true humour; and fatire, which is generally well directed : they are admirable
moral leffons, and afford a fund of entertainment fuited to every tafte : a cir-
cumftance, which fhews them to be juft
copies of nature. We may confider
them too as valuable repofitories of the
manners, cuftoms, and dreffes of the
prefent age. What amufement would
a collection of this kind afford, drawn
from every period of the hiftory of Bri-
tain ?—How far the works of HOGARTH
will bear a *critical examination,* may be
the fubject of a little more enquiry.

In *defign* HOGARTH was feldom at a
lofs. His invention was fertile ; and
his judgment accurate. An improper
incident

incident is rarely introduced; a proper one rarely omitted. No one could tell a ftory better; or make it, in all its circumftances, more intelligible. His genius, however, it muft be owned, was fuited only to *low*, or *familiar* fubjects. It never foared above *common* life : to fubjects naturally fublime; or which from antiquity, or other accidents borrowed dignity, he could not rife.

In *compofition* we fee little in him to admire. In many of his prints, the deficiency is fo great, as plainly to imply a want of all principle; which makes us ready to believe, that when we do meet with a beautiful group, it is the effect of chance. In one of his minor works, the *idle prentice*, we feldom fee a crowd more beautifully managed, than in the laft print. If the fheriff's officers had

not

nŏt been placed in a line, and had been brought a little lower in the picture, fo as to have formed a pyramid with the cart, the compofition had been unexceptionable: and yet the firft print of this work is fo ftriking an inftance of difagreeable compofition, that it is amazing, how an artift, who had any idea of beautiful forms, could fuffer fo unmafterly a performance to leave his hands.

Of the *diftribution of light* HOGARTH had as little knowledge as of *compofition.* In fome of his pieces we fee a good effect; as in the *execution* juft mentioned: in which, if the figures, at the right and left corners, had been *kept down* a little, the light would have been beautifully diftributed on the fore-ground, and a fine fecondary light fpread over part of the

the crowd: but at the fame time there is
fo obvious a deficiency in point of effect,
in moft of his prints, that it is very evi-
dent he had no principles.

Neither was HOGARTH a mafter in
drawing. Of the mufcles and anatomy
of the head and hands he had perfect
knowledge; but his trunks are often
badly moulded, and his limbs ill fet on.
I tax him with plain bad drawing; I
fpeak not of the niceties of anatomy,
and elegance of out-line: of thefe indeed he knew nothing; nor were they
of ufe in that mode of defign which he
cultivated: and yet his figures, upon
the whole, are infpired with fo much
life, and meaning; that the eye is kept
in good humour, in fpite of its inclina-
tion to find fault.

The

The author of the *Analyfis of Beauty*, it might be fuppofed, would have given us more inftances of *grace*, than we find in the works of HOGARTH; which fhews ftrongly that theory and practice are not always united. Many opportunities his fubjects naturally afford of introducing graceful attitudes; and yet we have very few examples of them. With inftances of *picturefque grace* his works abound.

Of his *expreffion*, in which the force of his genius lay, we cannot fpeak in terms too high. In every mode of it he was truly excellent. The paffions he thoroughly underftood; and all the effects which they produce in every part of the human frame: he had the happy art alfo of conveying his ideas with the fame precifion, with which he conceived them.—He was excellent too in expreff-

ing.

ing any humorous oddity, which we often
fee ftamped upon the human face. All
his heads are caft in the very mould of
nature. Hence that endlefs variety,
which is difplayed through his works:
and hence it is, that the difference arifes
between *his* heads, and the affected ca-
ricaturas of *thofe mafters,* who have fometimes amufed themfelves with patching
together an affemblage of features from
their own ideas. Such are SPANIOLET's;
which, tho admirably executed, appear
plainly to have no archetypes in nature.
HOGARTH's, on the other hand, are collections of natural curiofities. The *Ox-
ford-heads,* the *phyfician's-arms,* and fome
of his other pieces, are exprefly of this
humourous kind. They are truly co-
mic; tho ill-natured effufions of mirth:
more entertaining than SPANIOLET's, as
they

they are pure nature; but lefs innocent, as they contain ill-directed ridicule.—But the fpecies of expreffion, in which this mafter perhaps moft excels, is that happy art of catching thofe peculiarities of air, and gefture, which the ridiculous part of every profeffion contract; and which, for that reafon, become characte-riftic of the whole. His counfellors, his undertakers, his lawyers, his ufurers, are all confpicuous at fight. In a word, almoft every profeffion may fee in his works, that particular fpecies of affecta-tion, which they fhould moft endeavour to avoid.

The *execution* of this mafter is well fuited to his fubjects, and manner of treating them. He etches with great fpirit; and never gives one unneceffary ftroke. For myfelf, I greatly more va-lu

lue the works of his own needle, than
thofe high-finifhed prints, on which he
employed other engravers. For as the
production of an effect is not his talent;
and as this is the chief excellence of
high-finifhing ; his own rough manner is
certainly preferable ; in which we have
moft of the force, and fpirit of his expreffion. The *manner* in none of his
works pleafes me fo well, as in a fmall
print of a corner of a play-houfe. There
is more fpirit in a work of this kind,
ftruck off at once, warm from 'the imagination, than in all the cold correctnefs of an elaborate engraving. If all
his works had been executed in this
ftyle, with a few improvements in the
compofition, and the management of
light, they would certainly have been a
much more valuable collection of prints
than

than they are. The *Rake's progrefs*, and
fome of his other works, are both etched
and engraved by himfelf: they are well
done; but it is plain he meant them as
furniture. As works defigned for a cri-
tick's eye, they would certainly have
been better without the engraving ; except a few touches in a very few places.
The want of effect too would have been
lefs confpicuous, which in his higheft-fi-
nifhed prints is difagreeably ftriking.

CHAPTER

CHAPTER IV.

*Remarks on a few particular Prints, in the
several kinds of composition; with a view
to illustrate the observations, that have
been made above.*

THE RESURRECTION OF LARARUS; BY BLOEMART,

WITH regard to *design,* this print
has great merit. The point of
time is very judiciously chosen. It is a
point between the first command, *Lazarus come forth*; and the second, *Loose
him,*

him, and let him go. The aftonifhment of the two fifters is now over. The predominant paffion is gratitude; which is difcovering itfelf in praife. One of the attendants is telling the yet ftupified man, "That is your fifter." Himfelf, collecting his fcattered ideas, directs his gratitude to Chrift. Jefus directs it to heaven. So far the defign is good. But what are thofe idle figures on the right hand, and on the left? fome of them feem no way concerned in the action. Two of the principal are introduced as grave-diggers; but even in that capacity they were unwanted; *for the place,* we are told, *was a cave, and a ftone lay upon it.* When a painter is employed on a barren fubject, he muft make up his groups as he is able; but there is no barrennefs here:

the

the artift might, with propriety, have introduced, in the room of the grave-diggers, fome of the Pharifaical party maligning the action. Such, we are told, were on the fpot; and, as they are figures of confequence in the ftory, they ought not to have been fhoved back, as they are, among the appendages of the piece.

The *compofition* is almoft faultlefs. The principal group is finely difpofed. It opens in a beautiful manner, and dif-covers every part. It is equally beau-tiful, when confidered in combination with the figures on the left hand.

The *light* is but ill-diftributed, tho the figures are difpofed to receive the moft beautiful effect of it. The whole is one glare. It had been better, if all the figures on the elevated ground, on

N   the

the right, had been in ftrong fhadow.
The extended arm, the head and fhoulder of the grave-digger, might have received catching lights. A little more
light might have been thrown upon the
principal figure; and a little lefs upon
the figure kneeling. The remaining figures, on the left, fhould have been
kept down. Thus the light would have
centered ftrongly upon the capital group,
and would have faded gradually away.

The fingle figures are in general
good. The principal one indeed is not
fo capital as might be wifhed. The
character is not quite pleafing; the
right arm is aukwardly introduced, if
not ill-drawn; and the whole difagreeably incumbered with drapery.—Lazarus
is very fine: the drawing, the expreffion, and grace of the figure are all
good.

good.—The figure kneeling contrafts with the group.—The grave-diggers are both admirable. It is a pity, they fhould be incumbrances only.

The drawing is good; yet there feems to be fomething amifs in the pectoral mufcles of the grave-digger on the right. The hands too, in general, of all the figures, are conftrained and aukward. Few of them are in natural action.

The *manner*, which is mere ingraving, without any etching, is ftrong, diftinct, and expreffive.

THE

THE DEATH OF POLYCRATES; BY SALVATOR ROSA.

The *story* is well told: every part is fully engaged in the subject, and properly subordinate to it.

The *disposition* is agreeable. The contrivance of the groups, falling one into another, is very pleasing: and yet the form would have been more beautiful, if a ladder with a figure upon it, a piece of loose drapery, a standard, or some other object, had been placed on the left side of the cross, to have filled up that formal vacancy, in the shape of a right-angle, and to have made the pyramid more complete. The groups themselves are simple and elegant. The
three

three figures on horfeback indeed are bad. A line of heads is always unpleafing.

We have no ftrength of *keeping*. The whole is too much one furface; which might have been prevented by a little more force on the fore-ground, and a flighter fky.

The *light* is diftributed without any judgment. It might perhaps have been improved, if the group of the foldier refting upon his fhield, had been in fhadow; with a few catching lights. This fhadow, paffing through the label, might have extended over great part of the fore-ground above it: by which we fhould have had a body of fhadow to balance the light of the centre-group. The lower figures of the equeftrian-group might have received a middle

tint,

tint, with a few ftrong touches; the upper figures might have caught the light,
to detach them from the ground.——
There are fome lights too in the fky,
which would be better removed.

With regard to the figures taken feparately, they are almoft unexception-
ably good. You will feldom indeed fee
fo many good figures in any collection
of fuch a number. The young foldier
leaning over his fhield; the other figures of that group; the foldier point-
ing, in the middle of the picture; and
the figure behind him fpreading his
hands, are all in the higheft degree elegant, and graceful. The diftant figures
too are beautiful. The expreffion, in
the whole body of the fpectators, is very
ftriking. Some are more, and fome
lefs affected; but every one in a degree.

gree.——All the figures, however, are
not faultlefs. POLYCRATES hangs un-
gracefully upon his crofs: his body is
compofed of parallel lines, and right
angles. His face is ftrongly marked with
agony: but his legs are difproportioned
to his body. — The three lower figures
of the equeftrian-group have little beauty.——One of the equeftrian figures alfo,
that neareft the crofs, is formal and difgufting: and as to a horfe, SALVATOR
feems not to have had the leaft idea of
the proportion and anatomy of that animal.—Indeed the *whole* of this corner of
the print is bad; and I know not, whether the compofition would not be improved by the removal of it.

The fcenery is inimitable. The rock
broken, and covered with fhrubs at the
top; and afterwards fpreading into one
grand,

grand, and fimple fhade, is in itfelf a pleafing object; and affords an excellent back-ground to the figures.

The *execution* of this print is equal to that of any of SALVATOR'S works.

The triumph of Silenus; by Peter Testa.

P. Testa feems, in this elegant and mafterly performance, as far as his fublime ideas can be comprehended, to have intended a fatire on drunkennefs.

The *defign* is perfe&t. Silenus is introduced in the middle of the piece, holding an ivy-crown, and fupported by his train, in all the pomp of unwieldy majefty. Before him dance a band of bacchanalian rioters; fome of them, as defcribed by the poets,

——— inter pocula læti,
Mollibus in pratis, *un&tos faliere per utres.*

Intemperance, Debauchery, and unnatural Lufts complete the immoral feftival.

val. In the offſkip riſes the temple of
Priapus; and hard-by a mountain, dedi-
cated to lewdneſs, nymphs and ſatyrs.—
In the heavens are repreſented the *Moon*
and *Stars* puſhing back the *Sun:* imply-
ing, that ſuch revels, as are here deſcribed, dreaded the approach of day.

The *diſpoſition* has leſs merit; yet is
not unpleaſing. The group, on the
right of SILENUS, and the *ſeveral parts*
of it, are happily diſpoſed. The group
of dancers, on the other ſide, is crowded, and ill-ſhaped. The diſpoſition
might, perhaps, have had a better effect,
if an elegant canopy had been held over
SILENUS; which would have been no
improper appendage; and, by forming
the apex of a pyramid over the principal
figure, would have given more variety
and beauty to the whole.

The

The *light*, with regard to *particular figures*, is very beautiful. But such a light, at beft, gives you only the idea of a picture examined by a candle. Every figure, as you hold the candle to it, appears well lighted; but inftead of an *effect* of light, you have only a fucceffion of *fpots*. Indeed the light is not only ill, but abfurdly diftributed. The upper part is enlightened by one fun, and the lower part by another; the direction of the light being different in each.—Should we endeavour to amend it, it might be better perhaps to leave out the Sun; and to reprefent him, by his fymbols, as *approaching* only. The fky-figures would of courfe receive catching lights, and might be left nearly as they are. The figure of *Rain* under the *Moon* fhould be in fhadow.

The

The bear too, and the lion's head
fhould be *kept down.* Thus there.
would be nothing glaring in the celef-
tial figures. SILENUS, and his train,
might be enlightened by a very ftrong
torch-light, carried by the dancing figures. The light would then fall nearly as it does, upon the principal group.
The other figures fhould be *brought down*
to a middle tint. This kind of light
would naturally produce a gloom in the
back-ground, which would have a good
effect.

With regard to the figures taken feparately, they are conceived with fuch
claffical purity, and fimplicity of tafte ;
fo elegant in the drawing, and fo graceful in every attitude; that if I were obliged to fix upon any print, as an exam-
ple of all the beauties which fingle
figures

figures are capable of receiving, I fhould almoft be tempted to give the preference to this.

The moft ftriking inftances of fine *drawing* are feen in the principal figure; in the legs of the figure that fupports him; and in thofe of the figure dancing with the pipes; in the man and woman behind the centaur; in the figure in the clouds, with his right hand over his knee; in the Apollo; and particularly in that bold fore-fhortened figure of the fign Capricorn.

Inftances of *expreffion* we have in the unweildinefs of Silenus. He appears fo dead a weight, fo totally unelaftic, that every part of him, which is not fupported, finks with its own gravity. The fenfibility too with which his bloated body, like a quagmire, feels every touch,

touch, is ftrongly expreffed in his coun-
tenance. The figure, which fupports
him, expreffes in every mufcle the labour of the action. The dancing figures
are all ftrongly charaĉterized. The
pufhing figures alfo in the fky are
marked with great expreffion; and a-
bove all the threatening Capricorn, who
is reprefented in the act of drawing a bow.

With regard to *grace*, every figure,
at leaft every capital one, is agreeable;
if we except only that figure, which
lies kicking its legs upon the ground.
But we have the ftrongeft inftances of
grace in the figure dancing with the
pipes; in the man and woman behind
the centaur, (who, it is not improbable, might be defigned for Bacchus and
Ariadne;) and in the boy lying on the
ground.

With

With regard to *execution*, we rarely
fee an inftance of it in greater perfection. Every head, every mufcle, and
every extremity is touched with infinite
fpirit. The very appendages are fine;
and the ftone-pines, which adorn the
back-ground, are marked with fuch tafte
and precifion, as if landfcape had been
this artift's only ftudy.

SMITH's

Kneller, even when he laid himself out to excel, was often but a tawdry painter. His equestrian portrait of king William, at Hampton-court, is a very unmasterly performance: the composition is bad; the colouring gaudy; the whole is void of effect, and there is scarce a good figure in the piece.—The composition before us is more pleasing, tho' the effect is little better. An equestrian figure, at best, is an awkward subject. The legs of a horse are great encumbrances in grouping. Vandyke, indeed, has managed king Charles the First, on horse-back, with

with great judgment: and RUBENS too, at Hampton-court, has made a noble picture of the duke of ALVA; tho his horse is ill drawn.——In the print before us the figure fits with grace and dignity; but the horse is no Bucephalus: its character is only that of a managed pad. The bush, growing by the duke's truncheon, is a trifling circumstance; and helps to break, into more parts, a composition already too much broken.——The *execution* is throughout excellent; and tho the parts are rather too small for mezzotinto, yet SMITH has given them all their force.

O   PETHER's

Pether's mezzotinto of Rembrandt's Jewish rabbi.

The character is that of a ftern, haughty man, big with the idea of his own importance. The *rabbi* is probably fictitious ; but the *character* was certainly taken from nature. There is great dignity in it ; which in a work of REMBRANDT's is the more extraordinary.——The full expreffion of it is given us in the print. The unelaftic heaviness of age, which is fo well defcribed in the original, is as well preferved in the copy. The three equidiftant lights on the head, on the ornament, and on the hands, are difagreeable : in the print they

they could not be removed; but it might have been judicious to have *kept down* the two latter a little more.——With regard to the execution, every part is fcraped with the utmoft foftnefs, and delicacy. The mufcles are round and plump; and the infertions of them, which in an old face are very apparent, are well expreffed. Such a variety of middle tints, and melting lights, were difficult to manage; and yet they are managed with great tendernefs. The loofenefs of the beard is mafterly. The hands are exactly thofe of a fat old man. The ftern eyes are full of life; and the nofe and mouth are admirably touched. The feparation of the lips in fome parts, and adhefion in others, are characteriftic ftrokes; and happily preferved. The folds and lightnefs of the turban are ve-

O 2   ry

ry elegant. The robe, about the fhoulder, is unintelligible, and ill managed :
but this was the painter's fault.——In
a word, when we examine this very
beautiful mezzotinto, we muſt acknowledge, that no engraving can equal it
in foftneſs, and delicacy.

Hondius's hunted wolf.

The compofition, in this little print, is good; and yet there is too much fimilitude, in the direction of the bodies of the feveral animals. The group alfo is too much broken, and wants folidity. The horizon is taken too high; unlefs the dimenfions of the print had been higher. The rifing ground, above the wolf's head, had been offfkip enough: and yet the rock, which rifes higher, is fo beautifully touched; that it would be a pity to remove it.——The *light* is diftributed without any judgment. It might have been improved, if all the interftices among the legs, and heads of the animals, had been *kept down*; and the fhadow ſhadow made very ſtrong under the fawn, and the wounded dog. This would have given a bold relief to the figures; and might, without any other alteration, have produced a good effect. —The *drawing* is not faultleſs. The legs and body of the wounded dog are inaccurate : nor does the attacking dog ſtand firm upon his right leg.—With regard to *expreſſion*, HONDIUS has exerted· his full force. The expreſſion, both of the wounded dog, and of the wolf, is admirable : but the expreſſion of the attacking dog is a moſt bold and maſterly copy from nature. His attitude ſhews every nerve convulſed; and his head is a maſterpiece of animal fury.—We ſhould add, that the ſlaughtered animal is ſo ill-characterized, that we ſcarce know what it is.—

The

The *execution* is equal to the expreſſion.
It is neat, and highly finiſhed; but diſcovers in every touch the ſpirit of a
maſter.

THE FIFTH PLATE OF DU JARDIN'S
ANIMALS.

The *defign*, tho humble, is beautiful. The two dogs repofing at noon,
after the labour of the morning, the
implements of fowling, the fictitious
hedge, and the loop-holes through it,
all correfpond; and agreeably tell the
little hiftory of the day.——The *compofition* is beautiful: tho it might have
been improved; if another dog, or fomething equivalent, had been introduced
in the vacancy at the left corner. This
would have given the group of dogs a
better form. The nets, and fowling-
pieces are judicioufly added; and make
an agreeable fhape with the dogs. The
hedge

hedge alfo adds another pyramidal form; which would have been more pleafing if the left corner of the reeds had been a little higher.—The *light* is well diftri-buted; only there is too much of it. The farther dog might have been *taken down* a little; and the hinder parts of the nearer.——The *drawing* and *expref-fion* are pure nature; and the *execution* elegant and mafterly.

WATERLO'S

The landſcape I mean, is an upright
of the largeſt ſize, which this maſter e-
ver uſed; near twelve inches in height,
by ten. On the near ground ſtands an
oak, which forms a diagonal through
the print. The ſecond diſtance is compoſed of a riſing ground, connected with
a rock, which is covered with ſhrubs.
The oak, and the ſhrubs make a viſta,
through which you have an extenſive view
into the country. The figures, which
conſiſt of an angel, Tobias, and a dog,
are deſcending an hill, which forms the
ſecond diſtance. The print, with this
deſcription, cannot be miſtaken.—The
compoſition is very pleaſing. The trees,

on

on the fore-ground, fpreading over the
top of the print, and floping to a point
at the bottom, give the beautiful form
of an inverted pyramid; which, in trees
efpecially, has often a fine effect. To
this form the inclined plane, on which
the figures ftand, and which is beautifully broken, is a good contraft. The
rock approaches to a perpendicular, and
the diftance to an horizontal line. All
together make fuch a combination of
beautiful and contrafting lines, that
the whole is very pleafing. If I fhould
find fault with any thing, it is the regularity of the rocks. There is no variety
in parallels; and it had been very eafy
to have broken them.—The *keeping*
is well preferved. The fecond and third
diftances are both judicioufly managed.
The *light* is well difpofed. To prevent

vent heavineſs, it is introduced upon the tree, both at the top and at the bottom; but it is properly *kept down*. A maſs of ſhade ſucceeds upon the ground of the ſecond diſtance; and is continued upon the water. The light breaks, in a blaze, upon the bottom of the rock, and maſſes the *whole*. The trees, ſhrubs, and upper part of the rock are happily thrown into a middle tint. Perhaps the effect of the diſtant country might have been better, if all the lights upon it had been *kept down*; except one eaſy catching light upon the town, and the riſing ground on which it ſtands.—The *execution* is exceedingly beautiful. No artiſt had a happier manner of expreſſing trees than WATERLO; and the tree before us is one of his capital works. The ſhape of it we have already criticifed.

cifed. The bole and ramification are as beautiful as the fhape. The foliage is a mafterpiece. Such a union of ftrength, and lightnefs is rarely found. The extremities are touched with great tendernefs; the ftrong maffes of light are relieved with fhadows equally ftrong; and yet eafe, and foftnefs are preferved. The fore-ground is high-ly enriched; and indeed the whole print, and every part of it, is full of art, and full of nature.

The

THE DELUGE AT COEVERDEN, BY ROMAN LE HOOGHE.

This is an hiftorical landfcape, a ftyle very different from that of the laft. WATERLO had nothing in view, but to form an agreeable picture. He had all nature before him; through which his imagination might range. The figures, which he introduced, unconnected with his fubject, ferve only to embellifh it. Any other figures would have anfwered his defign as well. But LE HOOGHE was confined within narrower lines. He had a *country* to defcribe, and a *ftory* to tell. The *country* is the environs of Coeverden, a Dutch town, with a view of that immenfe bank, which the bifhop

of

of Munfter, in the year 1673, threw up, and fortified at a vaft expence, to lay the town under water. The *ftory,* is the ruin of that bank; which was broken through in three places, by the violence of a ftorm. The fubject was great and difficult; and yet the artift has acquitted himfelf in a mafterly manner. The town of Coeverden fills the diftant view. The country is fpread with a deluge; the fky with a tempeft; and the breaches in the bank appear in all their horror.—The *compofition,* in the diftant and middle parts, is as pleafing as fuch an extenfive fubject can be. An elevated horizon, which is always difgufting, was neceffary here to give a diftinct view of the whole.—The *light* too is thrown over the diftant parts in good maffes.—The *expreffion* of the fi-

gures,

gures, of the horfes efpecially, is very
ftrong: thofe, which the driver is turn-
ing, to avoid the horrid chafm before
him, are impreffed with the wildeft
character of terror: and, indeed, the
whole fcene of diftrefs, and the horri-
ble confufion in every part of it, are
admirably defcribed.—The *execution* is
good, tho not equal to that of many of
LE HOOGHE's works. It may be added, that the fhape of the print is bad.
A little more length would have enlarged the idea; and the town would
have ftood better, not quite in the middle.——But what is moft faulty, is the
difproportion, and littlenefs of the fore-
ground on the right. The fpirit, which
the artift had maintained through the
whole defcription, feems here to flag.
Whereas *here* he fhould have clofed the

whole

whole with fome noble confufion ; which would have given *keeping* to the diftant parts, and ftruck the fpectator with the ftrongeft images of horror. Inftead of this, we are prefented with a few pigs, and calves floundering in the water. The thought feems borrowed from Ovid. In the midft of a world in ruins, *Nat lupus inter oves.*

The firſt print of this capital work is
an excellent repreſentation of a young
heir, taking poſſeſſion of a miſer's effects.
The paſſion of avarice, which hoards
every thing, without diſtinction, what is
and what is not valuable, is admirably
deſcribed.—The *compoſition*, tho not excellent, is not unpleaſing. The principal group, confiſting of the young gentleman, the taylor, the appraiſer, the
papers, and cheſt, is well ſhaped : but
the eye is hurt by the diſagreeable regularity of three heads nearly in a line,
and at equal diſtances.——The *light* is
not ill diſpoſed. It falls on the principal figures : but the effect might have
been

been improved. If the extreme parts
of the mafs (the white apron on one
fide, and the memorandum-book on
the other) had been in fhade, the *repofe* had been lefs injured. The detached parts of a group fhould rarely catch
a ftrong body of light.—We have no
ftriking inftances of *expreffion* in this
print. The principal figure is unmeaning. The only one, which difplays the
true *vis comica* of HOGARTH, is the ap-
praifer fingering the gold. You enter
at once into his character.—The young
woman might have furnifhed the artift
with an opportunity of prefenting a
graceful figure; which would have been
more pleafing. The figure he *has* introduced, is by no means an object of
allurement.———The *perfpective* is accurate; but affected. So many win-

dows,

dows, and open doors, may fhew the author's learning; but they break the back ground, and injure the fimplicity of it.

The fecond print introduces our hero into all the diffipation of modifh life. We became firft acquainted with him, when a boy of eighteen. He is now of age; has entirely thrown off the clownifh fchool-boy; and affumes the man of fafhion. Inftead of the country taylor, who took meafure of him for his father's mourning, he is now attended by French-barbers, French-taylors, poets, milliners, jockies, bullies, and the whole retinue of a fine gentleman.—The *expreffion*, in this print, is wonderfully great. The dauntlefs front of the bully, the keen eye, and elafticity of the fencing-

fencing-mafter; and the fimpering importance of the dancing-mafter are admirably expreffed. The laft is perhaps
rather a little *outré.* The architect is a
ftrong copy from nature.——The *compofition* feems to be entirely fubfervient
to the expreffion. It appears, as if
HOGARTH had fketched, in his memorandum-book, all the characters which
he has here introduced; but was at a
lofs how to group them: and chofe rather to introduce them in detached
figures, as he had fketched them, than
to lofe any part of the expreffion by
combining them.—The *light* is ill diftributed. It is fpread indifcriminately
over the print; and deftroys the *whole.*—
We have no inftance of *grace* in any of
the figures. The principal figure is
very deficient. There is no contraft in
the

the, limbs; which is always attended with a degree of ungracefulnefs.—The *execution* is very good. It is elaborate, and yet free.—The fatire on operas, tho it may be well directed, is forced and unnatural.

The third plate carries us ftill deeper into the hiftory. We meet our hero engaged in one of his evening amufements. This print, on the whole, is no very extraordinary effort of genius.——The *defign* is good; and may be a very exact defcription of the humours of a brothel.—The *compofiticn* too is not amifs. But we have few of thofe mafterly ftrokes which diftinguifh the works of HOGARTH. The whole is plain hiftory. The lady fetting the world on fire, is the beft thought: and there is fome hu-

mour

mour in furnishing the room with a set
of Cæsars; and not placing them in
order. —— The *light* is ill managed.
By a few alterations, which are obvious, particularly by throwing the lady
dressing, into the shade, the disposition
of it might have been tolerable. But
still we should have had an absurdity to
answer, whence comes it? Here is
light in abundance; but no visible
source.——*Expression* we have very little through the whole print. That of
the principal figure is the best. The la-
dies have all the air of their profession;
but no variety of character. HOGARTH's
women are, in general, very inferior to
his men. For which reason I prefer the
rake's progress to the *harlot's*. The female face indeed has seldom strength of
feature

feature enough to admit the ftrong mark-
ings of expreffion.

Very difagreeable accidents often be-
fal gentlemen of pleafure. An event
of this kind is recorded in the fourth
print; which is now before us. Our
hero going, in full drefs, to pay his
compliments at court, on St. David's
day, was accofted in the rude manner
which is here reprefented.——The *compofition* is good. The form of the group,
made up of the figures in action, the
chair, and the lamp-lighter, is pleafing.
Only, here we have an opportunity of
remarking, that a group is difgufting
when the extremities of it are heavy.
A group in fome refpect fhould refemble a tree. The heavier part of the
foliage

foliage (the *cup*, as the landſcape-painter calls it) is always near the middle: the outſide branches, which are relieved by the ſky, are light and airy. An inattention to this rule has given a heavineſs to the group before us. The two bailiffs, the woman, and the chairman, are all huddled together in that part of the group which ſhould have been the lighteſt; while the middle part, where the hand holds the door, wants ſtrength and conſiſtence. It may be added too, that the four heads, in the form of a diamond, make an unpleaſing ſhape. All regular figures ſhould ſtudiouſly be avoided.——The *light* had been well diſtributed, if the bailiff holding the arreſt, and the chairman, had been a little lighter, and the woman darker. The glare of the white apron

apron is difagreeable. —— We have, in this print, fome beautiful inftances of *expreffion*. The furprife and terror of the poor gentleman is apparent in every limb, as far as is confiftent with the fear of difcompofing his drefs. The infolence of power in one of the bailiffs, and the unfeeling heart, which can jeft with mifery, in the other, are ftrongly marked. The felf-importance too of the honeft Cambrian is not ill portrayed; who is chiefly introduced to fettle the chronology of the ftory.—In point of *grace*, we have nothing ftriking. Ho-GARTH might have introduced a degree of it in the female figure; at leaft he might have contrived to vary the heavy and unpleafing form of her drapery.— The *perfpective* is good, and makes an agreeable fhape.———I cannot leave this

print

print without remarking the *falling band-
box*. Such reprefentations of quick motion are abfurd; and every moment the
abfurdity grows ftronger. You cannot deceive. the eye. The falling body *muſt* appear *not* to fall. Objects of
that kind are beyond the power of
reprefentation.

Difficulties crowd fo faft upon our
hero, that at the age of twenty-five,
which he feems to have attained in the
fifth plate, we find him driven to the
neceffity of marrying a woman, whom
he detefts, for her fortune. The *compofition* here is very good; and yet we
have a difagreeable regularity in the cli-
max of the three figures, the maid, the
bride, and the bridegroom.—The *light*
is not ill diftributed. The principal figure

gure too is *graceful*; and there is ftrong *expreffion* in the feeming tranquillity of his features. He hides his contempt of the object before him as well as he can; and yet he cannot do it. She too has as much meaning as can appear thro' the deformity of her features. The clergyman's face we are well acquainted with, and alfo his wig; tho we cannot pretend to fay, where we have feen either. The clerk too is an admirable fellow.——The *perfpective* is well underftood; but the church is too fmall; and the wooden poft, which feems to have no ufe, divides the picture very difagreeably.—— The creed loft, the commandments broken, and the poor's-box obftructed by a cobweb, are all excellent ftrokes of fatirical humour.

The

The fortune, which our adventurer
has juft received, enables him to make
one pufh more at the gaming table. He
is exhibited, in the fixth print, venting
curfes on his folly for having loft his laft
ftake.——This is upon the whole, perhaps, the beft print of the fet. The
horrid fcene it defcribes, was never more
inimitably drawn. The *compofition* is
artful, and natural. If the fhape of
the whole be not quite pleafing, the figures are fo well grouped, and with fo
much eafe and variety, that you cannot
take offence.—In point of light, it is
more culpable. There is not fhade e-
nough among the figures to balance the
glare. If the neck-cloth, and weepers
of the gentleman in mourning had been
removed, and his hands thrown into
fhade, even that alone would have improved

proved the effect.——The *expreſſion,* in
almoſt every figure, is admirable; and
the whole is a ſtrong repreſentation of
the human mind in a ſtorm. Three
ſtages of that ſpecies of madneſs, which
attends gaming, are here deſcribed. On
the firſt ſhock, all is inward diſmay.
The ruined gameſter is repreſented leaning againſt a wall, with his arms acroſs,
loſt in an agony of horror. Perhaps
never paſſion was deſcribed with ſo
much force. In a ſhort time this hor-
rible gloom burſts into a ſtorm of fury:
he tears in pieces what comes next him;
and kneeling down, invokes curſes upon himſelf. He next attacks others;
every one in his turn whom he imagines
to have been inſtrumental in his ruin.——
The eager joy of the winning game-
ſters, the attention of the uſurer, the
vehemence

vehemence of the watchman, and the profound revery of the highwayman, are all admirably marked. There is great coolnefs too expreffed in the little we fee of the fat gentleman at the end of the table. The figure oppofing the mad-man is bad : it has a drunken appearance; and drunkennefs is not the vice of a gaming table.——The principal figure is *ill drawn*. The *perfpective* is formal ; and the *execution* but indifferent : in heightening his expreffion HOGARTH has loft his fpirit.

The feventh plate, which gives us the view of a jail, has very little in it. Many of the circumftances, which may well be fuppofed to increafe the mifery of a confined debtor, are well contrived ; but the fruitful genius of HOGARTH, I

fhould

should think, might have treated the subject in a more copious manner. The episode of the fainting woman might have given way to many circumstances more proper to the occasion. This is the same woman, whom the rake discards in the first print; by whom he is rescued in the fourth; who is present at his marriage; who follows him into jail; and, lastly, to Bedlam. The thought is rather unnatural, and the moral certainly culpable.—The *composition* is bad. The group of the woman fainting, is a round heavy mass: and the other group is very ill shaped. The *light* could not be worse managed; and, as the groups are contrived, can hardly be improved.—In the principal figure there is great *expression*; and the fainting scene is well described.——A

scheme

fcheme to pay off the national debt, by
a man who cannot pay his own; and
the attempt of a filly rake, to retrieve
his affairs by a work of genius, are ad-
·mirable ftrokes of humour.

The eighth plate brings the fortunes
·of our hero to a conclufion. It is a ve-
·ry expreffive reprefentation of the moft
·horrid fcene which human nature can
·exhibit.————The *compofition* is not bad.
The group, in which the lunatic is
·chained, is well managed; and if it
had been carried a little further towards
the middle of the picture, and the two
women (who feem very oddly introduced) had been removed, both the com-
·pofition, and the diftribution of light
had been gcod.————The *drawing* of the
principal figure is a more accurate piece

Q   of

of anatomy than we commonly find in the works of this mafter. The *expref-fion* of the figure is rather unmeaning; and very inferior to the ftrong charac-ters of all the other lunatics. The fer-tile genius of the artift has introduced as many of the caufes of madnefs, as he could well have collected; but there is fome tautology. There are two religio-nifts, and two aftronomers. Yet there is variety in each; and ftrong *expreffion* in all the characters. The felf-fatisfac-tion, and conviction, of him who has difcovered the longitude; the mock majefty of the monarch; the moody melancholy of the lover; and the fuper-ftitious horror of the popifh devotée, are all admirable.—The *perfpective* is fimple and proper.

I fhould

I fhould add, that thefe remarks are made upon the firft edition of this work. When the plates were much worn, they were altered in many parts. They have gained by the alterations, in point of *defign*; but have loft in point of *exprefffion*.

CHAPTER V.

CAUTIONS IN COLLECTING PRINTS.

THE collector of prints may be
first cautioned against indulging a
desire of becoming possessed of *all* the
works of any master. There are no
masters whose works in the *gross* deserve
notice. No man is equal to himself in
all his compositions. I have known a
collector of REMBRANDT ready to give
any price for two or three prints which

he

he wanted to complete his collection; tho it had been to REMBRANDT's credit, if thofe prints had been fuppreffed. There is no doubt, but if one third of the works of this mafter fhould be tried by the rules of juft criticifm, they would appear of little-value. The great prince *Eugene,* it is faid, was a collector of this kind; and piqued himfelf upon having in his poffeffion, *all the works of all the mafters.* His collection was bulky, and coft fourfcore thoufand pounds; but when fifted, could not, at that time of day, be worth fo many hundreds.

The collector of prints may fecondly be cautioned againft a fuperftitious veneration for names. A true judge leaves the *mafter* out of the queftion, and examines only the *work.* But, with a little
genius,

genius, nothing fways like a name. It carries a wonderful force; covers glaring faults, and creates imaginary beauties. That fpecies of criticifm is certainly juft, which examines the different manners of different mafters, with a view to difcover in how many ways a good effect may be produced, and which produces the beft. But to be curious in finding out a mafter, in order *there* to reft the judgment, is a kind of criticifm very paltry, and illiberal. It is judging of the work by the mafter, inftead of judging of the mafter by the work. Hence it is, that fuch vile prints as the *Woman in the caldron*, and *Mount Parnaſſus*, obtain credit among connoiffeurs. If you afk wherein their beauty confifts? you are informed, they are engraved by MARK ANTONIO: and

if

if that do not fatisfy you, you are further affured, they are after RAPHAEL.
This abfurd tafte raifed an honeft indig-
nation in that ingenious artift PICART:
who having fhewn the world, by his excellent imitations, how ridiculous it is to
pay a blind veneration to *names*; tells
us, that he had compared fome of the
engravings of the ancient mafters with
the original pictures ; and found them
very bad copies. He fpeaks of the ftiffnefs, which in general runs through
them——of the hair of children, which
refembles pot-hooks—and of the igno-
rance of thofe engravers in anatomy,
drawing, and the diftribution of light.

Nearly allied to this folly, is that of
making the public tafte our ftandard.
It is a moft uncertain criterion. Fafhion
prevails

prevails in every thing. While it is confined to drefs, or the idle ceremonies of
a vifit, the affair is trivial: but when
fafhion becomes a dictator in arts, the
matter is more ferious. Yet fo it is;
we feldom permit ourfelves to judge of
beauty by the rules of art: but follow
the catch-word of fafhion; and applaud,
and cenfure from the voice of others.
Hence it happens, that fometimes the
works of one mafter, and fometimes of
another, have the prevailing run. REM-
BRANDT has long been the fafhionable
mafter. Little diftinction is made: if
the prints are REMBRANDT's, they muft
be good. In two or three years more,
perhaps, the date of REMBRANDT will
be over: you may buy his works at eafy
rates; and the public will have acquired
fome other favourite. For the truth of
thefe

thefe obfervations, I might appeal to the dealers in old prints; all of whom know the uncertain value of the commodity they vend. Hence it is, that fuch noble productions, as the works of P. Testa, are in fuch little efteem, that the whole collection of this mafter, tho it confifts of near twenty capital prints, befide many fmall ones, may be bought for lefs than is fometimes given for a fingle print of Rembrandt. The true connoiffeur leaves the voice of fafhion entirely out of the queftion: he has a better ftandard of beauty — the merit of each mafter, which he will find frequently at variance with common opinion.

A fourth caution, which may be of ufe in collecting prints, is, not to rate their

their value by their *fcarcenefs*. Scarce-
nefs will make a *valuable* print *more valuable*: but to make fcarcenefs the ftandard of a print's value, is to miftake an
accident for merit. This folly is founded in vanity; and arifes from a defire
of poffeffing what nobody elfe can poffefs. The want of *real* merit is made
up by *imaginary*; and the object is intended to be *kept*, nor *looked at*. Yet,
abfurd as this falfe tafte is, nothing is
more common; and a trifling genius may
be found, who will give ten guineas for
HOLLAR's fhells, which, valued according to their merit (and much merit they
certainly have) are not worth more
than twice as many fhillings.—Inftances
in abundance might be collected of the
prevalence of this folly. LE CLERC,
in his print of *Alexander's triumph*, had
given

given a profile of that prince. The print was shewn to the duke of Orleans; who was pleafed with it on the whole, but juftly enough objected to the fide-face. The obfequious artift erafed it, and engraved a full one. A few impreffions had been taken from the plate in its firft ftate ; which fell among the curious for ten times the price of the impreffions taken after the face was altered.——CALLOT, once pleafed with a little plate of his own etching, made a hole in it; through which he drew a ribbon, and wore it at his button. The impreffions after the hole was made, are very fcarce, and amazingly valuable.—— In a print of the holy family, from VANDYKE, St. John was reprefented laying his hand upon the virgin's fhoulder. Before the print was publifhed, the

the artift fhewed it among his critical
friends, fome of whom thought the action of St. John too familiar. The painter was convinced, and removed the
hand. But he was miftaken, when he
thought he added value to his print by
the alteration. The few impreffions,
which got abroad, with the hand upon
the fhoulder, would buy up all the reft,
three times over, in any auction in London.—Many of REMBRANDT's prints receive infinite value from little accidental
alterations of this kind, A few impreffions were taken from one plate, before
a dog was introduced; from another,
before a white horfe-tail was turned into
a black one; from a third, before a
fign-poft was inferted at an ale-houfe
door: and all the fcarce prints from
thefe plates, tho altered for the better,
                                        are

are the prints of value: the reſt are common and cheap.—I ſhall conclude theſe inſtances with a ſtory of a late celebrated collector of pictures. He was ſhewing his collection with great ſatisfaction; and after expatiating upon many noble works by GUIDO, MARRATTI, and other maſters, he turned ſuddenly to the gentleman, whom he attended, and, " Now, Sir, ſaid he, I'll ſhew you a real curioſity: there is a WOVERMAN without a horſe in it."—The circumſtance, it is true, was uncommon; but was unluckily that very circumſtance, which made the picture of little value.

Let the collector of prints be cautioned, fifthly, to beware of buying copies for originals. Moſt of the works of the capital maſters have been copied; and

many

many of them fo well, that if a perfon be not verfed in prints, he may eafily be deceived. Were the copies really as good as the originals, the name would fignify nothing: but, like tranf-lations, they neceffarily fall fhort of the fpirit of the original; and contraⅆ a ftiffnefs from the fear of erring. When feen apart, they look well; but when compared with the originals, the difference eafily appears. Thus CALLOT's *beggars* have been fo well copied, that the difference between the originals and the copies would not immediately ftrike you; but when you compare them, it is obvious. There is a plain want of freedom; the charaⅆers are lefs ftrongly marked; and the extremities are lefs accurately touched.——It is a difficult matter to give rules to affift in diftin-

guifhing

guiſhing the copy from the original. In moſt caſes the engraver's name, or his mark (which ſhould be well known) will be a ſufficient direction. Theſe the copyiſt is ſeldom hardy enough to forge. But in anonymous prints it is matter of more difficulty. All that can be done, is to attend carefully to the *freedom* of the *manner*, in the *extremities* eſpecially, in which the copyiſt is more liable to fail. When you are pretty well acquainted with the *manner* of a maſter, you cannot well be deceived. When you are not, your beſt way is to be directed by thoſe who are.

The laſt caution I ſhall give to the collector of prints, is, to take care he purchaſe not bad impreſſions.—There are three things which make an impreſ-
ſion

fion bad.—The firft is, its being *ill taken off*. Some prints feem to have received the force of the roller at intervals. The impreffion is double; and gives that glimmering appearance, which illudes the eye. —— A fecond thing, which makes an impreffion bad, is *a worn plate*. There is as much difference between the firft and the laft impreffion of the fame plate, as between two different prints. The *effect* is wholly loft in a faint impreffion; and you have nothing left but a vapid defign without fpirit, and without force. In mezzotinto, efpecially, a ftrong impreffion is defireable. For the fpirit of a mezzotinto quickly evaporates; without which it is the moft infipid of all prints. In engraving and etching there will be always, here and there, a dark touch, which

R   long

long preferves an appearance of fpirit:
but mezzotinto is a flat furface; and
when it begins to wear, it wears *all
over*. Very many of the works of all
the great mafters, which are commonly
hawked about at auctions, or fold in
fhops, are in this wretched ftate. It is
difficult to meet with a good impreffion.
The SALVATORS, REMBRANDTS, and
WATERLOS, which we meet with now,
except here and there in fome choice
collection, are feldom better than mere
reverfes. You fee the form of the print;
but the elegant, and mafterly touches
are gone; back-grounds and fore-
grounds are jumbled together by the
confufion of all diftance.; and you have
rather the fhadow of a print left, than
the print itfelf.—The laft thing which
makes a bad impreffion, is the *retouching*

of

of a worn plate. Sometimes this is performed by the master himself; and then the spirit of the impression may be tolerably preserved. But most commonly the retouching part is done by some bungler, into whose hands the plate may have fallen; and then it is execrable. In a *worn* plate, at least, what you have is good: you have the remains of something excellent; and if you are versed in the works of the master, your imagination may be agreeably exercised in making out what is lost. But when the plate has gone through the hands of a bungler, who has worked it over with his infamous scratches, the idea of the master is lost; and you have nothing left, but strong, harsh, and umeaning lines upon a faint ground; which is the most disagreeable compound with which the

eye

eye can be prefented. Such prints, and many fuch there are, though offered us under the name of Rembrandt, or Waterlo, are of little value. Thofe mafters would not have owned them. —Yet, as we are often obliged to take up with fuch impreffions as we can get, let us rather chufe the *faint* impreffion, than the *retouched* one.

THE END.

I N D E X.

INDEX.

INDEX.

INDEX.

I N D E X.

INDEX.

O

INDEX.

S

I N D E X.

INDEX.